THEY DARED TO BE DIFFERENT

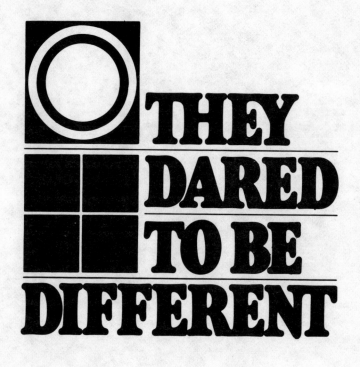

THEY
DARED
TO BE
DIFFERENT

HARVEST HOUSE PUBLISHERS
Irvine, California 92714

THEY DARED TO BE DIFFERENT

Copyright © 1976 Harvest House Publishers
Irvine, California 92714
Library of Congress Catalog Card Number: 76-42174
ISBN-0-89081-029-X

Printed in the United States of America

Appreciation

For more than ten years I watched, waited and prayed for Ken and Elaine Jacobs as they, with a melange of pain, bewilderment, frustration and joy, midwifed the Chamula church.

The years passed and many requested Ken's permission to write the Chamula story. With his usual good-naturedness Ken politely said, "No, the time is not right, but when it is, I've promised that Hugh Steven should write the story." For this high privilege and honor I now thank him.

To Mariano, for his patience and willingness to share his life.

For the many who helped, prayed and encouraged.

To Dr. Benjamin Elson who first commissioned me to

write the story, and to Clarence Church, Director of Wycliffe's Home Division, who encouraged me to write the story as I truly felt it.

To Danny O'Brien and Mary Jo McMahon, Wycliffe's editorial staff, Dr. Marvin Mayers, Professor of Anthropology, and Dr. George Cowan, President of Wycliffe Bible Translators, who read the manuscript and offered helpful suggestions.

I am especially grateful to Tugrul Uke, a special friend of the Jacobs and former resident of Las Casas, for permission to use his data and background material for "the cutting hour" chapter.

Lastly to Norma, my wife, who continues to be my indispensable companion in writing for the glory of God.

Hugh Steven

Table of Contents

Introduction 9

Glossary 10

Chapter 1   The Man with the Mouth 13

Chapter 2   Death and Dreams 25

Chapter 3   Happiness and Heartbreak 37

Chapter 4   Hurt, Hate and Hope 51

Chapter 5   The Cutting Hour 63

Chapter 6   I Want Her! 75

Chapter 7   Let It Be Thus 87

Chapter 8   The Helper 101

Chapter 9   It Will Stay By Means of Me 115

Chapter 10 It Is with One Heart I Sleep 129

Chapter 11 You Make That Choice 141

Chapter 12 In the Process of Succeeding 155

Introduction

For the most part the "people of the mud," as the ancient Aztecs dubbed the robust Chamula people of Mexico's Chiapas highlands, conform to their prescribed social mold. Yet in every age, in every society, there are always some who, though not fully understanding why, choose to challenge the presuppositions of tradition.

This is the true story of those who dared to challenge the status quo. It's the story of those who felt the searing pains of their own spiritual rebirth. And it's the story of Mariano who found he not only battled the traditions of the elders but also the hot passions of his mind and body.

Glossary

atole	—	corn meal gruel
brujo	—	literally "a giver of sickness and death," considered to be a bad witch doctor
cabildo	—	town hall
cabrón	—	literally "he-goat," an offensive epithet roughly equivalent to "bastard"
cashlan	—	outsider
chamarra	—	heavy, sleeveless, knee-length, homespun tunic
gringo	—	American
ilol	—	literally "a sayer of words"
ladino	—	a westernized, Spanish-speaking Latin American
mayols	—	policemen
milpa	—	a small field cleared from the jungle
posh	—	sugar cane rum
Vinahel	—	final resting place

Chapter

1

THE MAN
WITH THE
MOUTH

The Man with the Mouth

He walked into the church courtyard, paused, looked carefully at three small children playing marbles in the dust, then sat down on a cement tile bench. The iron arm and back rests had been bent and broken long ago, but he didn't care. He had hiked most of the 40 miles from the ancient city of Chiapa de Corzo at 1,200 feet to the city of San Cristobal de las Casas at 7,200 feet and he was tired.

Yet it was more than fatigue and his hot burning feet which caused him to rest. It was fear! He needed time to think. Once he entered Chamula territory and especially the town and ceremonial center of San Juan Chamula he knew Mexican law ended and Chamula tribal law began.

"Ah, those cursed laws and traditions," he thought as he ground down hard on his stubby, tobacco-stained teeth. "Damn the law of conformity. Why wouldn't the council of elders listen? Why wouldn't they open their ears to my suggestions? If they had I would have been president and would still live with my wife and son in the hills above San Juan Chamula." Slowly he lowered his head into his thick calloused hands, closed his eyes, and remembered . . . .

It was several nights before the ceremonial washing, before he was to be installed as president over 118 settlements. He with several members of the town hierarchy shuffled into the adobe *cabildo* in San Juan Chamula. All wore traditional Chamula garb—thick, nail-studded, leather sandals; grey-white, calf-length pantaloons made from heavy, unbleached cotton; and medium-crown, straw sombreros. Over this, each wore a black ceremonial *chamarra*. Some of the men also wore a large fringed handkerchief which covered their heads and hats.

Then, as if guided by inner sonar, the men formed a semicircle according to an unspoken rank. Among them were town elders, *mayordomos*—those who served the holy images, dressing and taking them out on special festival days, bellringers, and *mayols*, with their heavy black oak clubs. It was the *mayols'* job to run errands for the president and arrest all dissidents.

In silence, all faced an older man with a long, silver-knobbed staff in his hand. He sat expressionless behind a crude, hand-fashioned, pine table. He was the outgoing president, the "man with the mouth." For the past year he had been responsible to guard and execute all of San Juan Chamula's community and religious activities. Only when all eyes were fixed on him did he speak.

''Give the *posh* to the youngest man,'' he said.

Like all officials before him, the president-elect would serve the presidency without remuneration. It was his responsibility to supply the *posh* for this occasion and from under his *chamarra* he pulled a large bottle of locally distilled rum.

Posh is not only the focal point for the whole cycle of Chamula life but is also part of their ancient Mayan heritage. Chamulas drink because they believe *posh* is holy medicine, a prerequisite to heaven. And they drink because no one can stand to live in isolation. If a Chamula by some strange creative twist decides to be his own man and not drink, he is immediately suspect. ''If he doesn't drink,'' reasons the president and council of elders, ''he doesn't think like us and cannot be a part of us.'' In some cases such a person is considered a dissident and if he is a dissident he is an enemy, and all enemies must die.

Instinctively most Chamulas understand these unwritten laws and silently allow the president and council of elders to make all decisions of conscience. The pressure to conform and submit to tradition far outweighs any loss of personal integrity or physical indebtedness. For this president-elect the indebtedness he would incur to supply the *posh* was a small price to pay for the prestige of becoming the man with the mouth. As president he would wield heady power. He was *the* man to guide 50,000 Chamulas through their ceremonial and religious life. And when his term was over he would automatically become an officer in the most powerful and prestigious of all offices—the council of elders.

After giving the *posh* to the youngest man who served the others in order of rank, they all waited until the president had been served his shot of *posh*. Holding it in his left hand, the president bowed, then raised his glass to offer a toast. Beginning with the highest ranking male, the president said, "Take your drink." He then called that man by his family name. In response the man said, "I drink." When all toasts were completed, the president drank his *posh* in one healthy gulp, grimaced to show how strong the liquor was, spit a few drops on the floor, and stuck out his glass for a refill.

It was during the seventh round of the drinking ceremony, when eyes were beginning to glaze and tongues thicken, that the president-elect made his fatal error.

"Old and younger brothers," he said, "we all know how scarce is our land and how small our farms, how all must work on the *cashlan's* coffee plantations to earn enough money for our needs, why not make the *cashlan* work for us? For once let him give us money."

If he had not been quite so full of *posh* he would have noticed the raised eyebrows and wrinkled foreheads and stopped talking. But the importance of his upcoming office was hot in his veins. Each man held his breath and for an instant stood frozen. Eager to impress his peers, he didn't hear the older men suck in their breath as he continued with his new idea. "Since all Chamulas live on their own *milpas* away from San Juan Chamula, let us rent that unused land near the *cabildo* to a *cashlan*. Let him pay us to farm it. The money can buy more *posh*."

With his head buried in his hands, the former president-elect cursed the memory of his words and remembered the events of the night he fled for his life. The night old Juan came to his house.

"Are you there, my younger brother?"

"Ah, Juan, yes I am here, my older brother. Come into my house. What is the purpose of your visit?"

"There is no purpose, younger brother. I've come only to sit and drink *posh* with you."

But there had to be a purpose. No Chamula ever visited another without a reason. The president-elect knew this and felt uneasy. Old Juan sensed the uneasiness but played his Judas role flawlessly.

"Younger brother," he said smoothly, "we of the council are happy you will soon be our new president. Here, drink our holy *posh*."

The plan was simple. Juan knew once the president-elect accepted the *posh* it would bind their friendship and whatever he had come for. He would get him drunk; then, on signal, the men who were now silently surrounding the house, would rush through the door and kill the president-elect with their long humpback machetes and loaded single-shot muskets.

A master of deceit, old Juan tried to allay his host's fears and fed his ego by telling him what an important man he was soon to become and how much power he would have later on as a council member. But as the two men squatted on low wooden stools which looked like tunnels from a child's electric train set, the president-elect still felt something was wrong and after each glass of *posh*, nervously jumped up and peered outside.

Just as he was beginning to think he had nothing to

fear, he thought he saw a man in a white *chamarra*. Without giving a thought to old Juan, he scrambled into his attic to look out a larger window. What he saw made his heart freeze, but not his legs. With a single bound, he jumped from the attic and burst through the door into a circle of twenty Chamula men all clad in white *chamarras* and all eager to slay him!

His unexpected action confused the would-be assassins. There was much yelling, flailing of razor-sharp machetes overhead, and unorganized commands to kill. But the Chamula killers were in a small circle and hesitated to strike out in the dark for fear of killing one of their own men. It was in that instant the president-elect slipped through their grasp and fled into the night like a highland rabbit.

The former president-elect lifted his head from his hands and watched the small boys playing marbles. Each scuffed and slid around the periphery of their dirt circle looking for the best angle to shoot out their opponent's marble.

He watched two teenage Indian girls giggle and laugh flirtatiously with an Indian youth. He thought of his wife. He thought of his son. And he made up his mind.

"After all," he reasoned, "it's been over two years since it happened. Two new presidents have been elected. Many of those who plotted my murder will be out of office. Besides, who will remember such a minor break with Chamula tradition?"

But the years away working in the outsider's coffee plantation absorbing their cultural values had softened his understanding of Chamula tradition. He failed to remember Chamulas never forget or forgive!

Slowly he pulled himself together and made his way toward the central market. There were always trucks hauling sugar cane into San Juan Chamula for at least one of the nearly 600 clandestine stills. He would beg a ride.

As he walked over the smooth cobblestone streets of San Cristobal de las Casas, the old familiar sights began to attract his senses. He passed a young boy selling peanuts. An old woman with matted, disheveled hair pointed to her carved wooden basins and footstools. Behind a cracked and sagging adobe wall he heard the rhythmic pat-a-pat of someone making tortillas. The sound and stimulative mixture of garlic and herb smells tickled his saliva glands. At one street the cobblestones stopped and he walked around a deep rut filled with slime-green water and a half-submerged banana peel. He passed an old man with a thick cane who looked at him quizzically out of one eye.

He came to a stall where a vendor sold only onions and cabbages; passed another with chicken gizzards and little bundles of yellow chicken feet displayed on a plank held up by two soda pop cases. The attendant was an old woman who swooshed away the flies with a whisk made from dirty strips of cloth tacked to a short wooden handle stained dull-red from chicken blood.

Each step closer to the truck filled him with renewed confidence and determination to end his exile. He loved his land, his Tzotzil language, and in spite of all that had happened, was proud to be from the town of San Juan Chamula.

He knew about the 27 other Tzotzil-speaking townships in the highlands of Chiapas. Each spoke a distinct dialect of the Tzotzil language—a branch of the once great Maya-Quiche language family. And each had its own ceremonial center, church, and patron saint. Yet for all their similarity his people remain an ethnic island. Almost no inter-township marriages occur.

A curious outsider once asked him why this was so. He smiled and shrugged his shoulders. He knew, but he didn't want the outsider to know. How could he tell an outsider that all Chamulas believe themselves to be superior to all other Tzotzils, and they are certainly superior to all *ladino* or *gringo cashlans*.

It was with this same feeling of superiority and a little arrogance that he jumped from the deck of the dual-wheel Dodge truck when it stopped at Kilometer 87, a half hour walk to San Juan Chamula. His jump was heavy, flat footed, like he intended to stamp out a grass fire. With a mumbled ''gracias'' to the driver, he watched the truck disappear down the Pan-American Highway.

With strong, measured steps he set out for his own one-room, thatched-roof house in the hills above San Juan Chamula. His reason for returning was not entirely to be reunited with his family. True, he missed his wife, but not in the same way a *gringo cashlan* might miss his wife. There were always women available near the plantations. He also missed his son. He was proud to have a male heir. But he missed the fiestas more, that sense of belonging and the deep obligation he felt to honor the dead of his family. It was for this reason he chose to return on All Saint's Day, the first day of November and the eve of the Day of the Dead.

When he appeared at his doorway and kicked out at a rib-lined cur of a dog who yelped his arrival, his wife immediately reminded him of his duty.

"Woman, I am back," he said.

"I see you are, man," she said with no emotion. "It is good you have come. We need candles and *posh* from the market."

"And my son?"

"He is well. He does the work of a man. He tends our garden. Even now he does your work and cleans the weeds from the graves of our families."

"And what of the path?"

"Yes, he has marked a path in the direction of our house. The souls of your mother and father will not become lost. They will know the house where they lived and died."

"And what of the food?"

"I have cleaned the special bowl for soup with cabbage and meat. And the one for the unsweetened *atole*. I have the plate of salt but we yet lack candles and *posh*.

"I will call my son. Then we two together will go to San Juan Chamula."

Chapter

2

DEATH
AND
DREAMS

Death and Dreams

Few in the large crowd who gathered that morning in the plaza of San Juan Chamula for the festival of All Saints noticed one of the *mayols* sprinkle kerosene on a bundle of dry thatch grass near the *cabildo*. Everyone concentrated on their preparation to honor the spirits of their dead relatives. This was a time for all to feast and get drunk. All, that is, except the council, president, and *mayols*. They had work to do.

Even before he entered the large, bare, treeless plaza, an alert *mayol* informed the council, president, and other *mayols* that the former president-elect had returned. They had not forgotten he was a dissident and as if it had been rehearsed every day for two years, they began to execute their plan.

The former president-elect saw the smoke and heard the crowd yell, "Fire! Fire!" but he was too far from the *cabildo* to see exactly what was burning. His son ran to see but he thought only of the *posh* and candles he was to buy.

The first hint that the fire might concern him came from the shopkeeper where he bought his candles.

"Look," said the shopkeeper, "the *mayols*."

"What of them? They are always here at festival time."

"Yes, yes, I know. But they come here and point to you!"

"Greetings, older brother," said a grinning *mayol*. "It is a bad thing you do on the first day of your return."

"What do you mean I do a bad thing? I have just now come to our plaza."

"It is no small thing, older brother, to set a fire to the *cabildo*."

"*Cabrón!*" screamed the former president-elect. "How could I set fire to the *cabildo*? I am here and have not even come close by to it."

"*Cabrón*, yourself," gloated the *mayol*. "Tell all your lies to the president."

He wanted to run but the *mayols*, anticipating his move, surrounded and quickly grabbed him. Then while he screamed rough epithets and proclaimed his innocence, the *mayols* dragged him past the *cabildo* and tied him at ground level to a Mayan cross outside the church courtyard.

With mute satisfaction the new president and council of San Juan Chamula watched passersby laugh and taunt the former president-elect. And when the president finally confronted him, it was with the same mocking attitude.

"Why is it, older brother, that you want to burn down our *cabildo*?"

"Esteemed president, how could I be the one to start such a fire? I was never close to the *cabildo*."

"You lie, older brother, and deserve to die."

"Die? What have I done that death should come by me?"

"You, older brother, should die because you are no longer one with the traditions of our ancestors. Your soul is not the same as ours."

Swearing under his breath, the former president-elect strained at the thongs which cut into his wrists. In frustration he shook his head from side to side. "That is a lie," he pleaded. "Look at me. I wear the *chamarra*. I speak our language. Have I not returned to honor our patron saint San Juan? Have I not prepared to honor and feed the souls of my ancestors? And do I not drink our holy *posh*?"

"And is it not true, older brother, you wanted us to learn what you learned from the outside? Did you not want to admit the *ladino cashlan* to farm our land? And do you not forget a true Chamula is superior to all other peoples? That he is faithful to all the traditions and laws of the council of elders whatever those laws might be?"

The former president-elect knew there was no hope of ever persuading the new president not to have him killed if for no other reason than to demonstrate his power. Yet there was one last glimmer of hope and he grasped it like a drowning man.

"Esteemed president, I want to be judged in Las Casas. Let the *cashlan* decide if I have guilt."

"All right, dissident brother. If you want *cashlan* justice, that is what you will get." With a disgusted flick of his hand, the president ordered the *mayols* to untie him and take him to Las Casas.

The former president-elect smiled smugly, rubbed his wrists, and walked out of the plaza of San Juan Chamula in the company of six club-carrying *mayols*. "I might not be able to persuade the *cashlans* of my innocence," he thought, "but at least they will not kill me."

But the *mayols* had their orders.

All walked in silence to a short distance from the plaza where the trail narrowed between two high hills. Suddenly the *mayols*, certain no one could see them, began to yell, "The dissident brother escapes! Stop him! Stop him!"

And they did. The shadows were long and fell sharply along the canyon walls, and so did the clubs. Again and again they clubbed him until, blood-spattered, he lay still, dead in the dirt.

But someone had seen them. The former president-elect's son had followed behind. As the *mayols* stopped to clean their blood-stained clubs before going back to the plaza, they heard a small voice cry, "Daddy, Daddy!" Suddenly they were faced with another tribal responsibility, and they left the boy beside his father—dead.

Five-year-old Mariano Gomez Hernandez knew this story as well as he knew his own name and that he was Chamula—one of the "real" people. It had been told and retold in his hearing by his mother. Usually this occurred when Mariano's father, Miguel, was drunk and slurred the imposed unattainable ideals of a new president or council. When it came to the clubbing part of the story, Mariano's mother forced home her point by clenching her right hand and slapping it into her open left hand. Mariano trembled with fear when his mother did this. But then Mariano was always afraid. As a child there never seemed to be a time when he wasn't afraid.

He was afraid of his father who frequently pushed aside Mariano's grandmother from the food circle. "Get away, old woman, you eat too much," he would say. Mariano's mother always countered with, "Man, why do you refuse a small bowl of thin cabbage soup and an extra tortilla to my mother?"

"Why should she eat?" Mariano's father would say. "She doesn't watch the sheep. She can't hoe the *milpa* or harvest corn."

"My mother gathers firewood and looks after your son!"

Miguel's response was always the same. "Ha, the firewood she gathers is nothing but twigs. And as for that *cabrón* of a son, he is like a stupid goat. Aren't you a stupid goat, Mariano?"

Often too afraid to answer, Mariano would remain silent. When he did, he felt a thunking cuff on the side of his head. Sobbing, he would find comfort in his grandmother's lap or by running outdoors to the sheep pen.

Mariano's mother shared some of her husband's heartless attitudes toward her son yet often screamed at Miguel, "Drunken pig! We have so little food because you drink too much *posh*. Add also to your shame that your son tells his grandmother he is cold and is ashamed to play wearing only a torn shirt. By this time all fathers have provided their sons with pantaloons and a warm *chamarra*.''

Humiliated and unable to counter his wife's verbal attacks, Miguel, to the horror of his three daughters and son, would beat his wife across the buttocks with the flat side of his machete. The old grandmother would say nothing. She remembered her own beatings. It was part of Chamula life.

Besides the fear of his father, Mariano was afraid of his Uncle Domingo. Uncle Domingo was an *ilol* and it was to him that people in the settlement came when there was sickness, crop failure, or when an angry ancestral god needed to be appeased.

No one could ever be sure when they might have done something to offend one of the gods. Only an *ilol* by "touching the blood" (feeling the pulse of a patient at the wrist and elbow, first on the right, then on the left), could understand and interpret why a person was ill or his crops had failed.

"It is because the blood talks," explained his grandmother to Mariano one day. "The blood talks and sends messages which only an *ilol* can understand." It was this worry of offending a god or going too close to where they lived, plus the worry of falling, which caused Mariano his deepest fear.

"The most dangerous thing you can do is fall," warned his grandmother repeatedly. "When you play or hunt little birds, never do so near the waterspring. It is in this way your soul could be lost. If you fall near to the place where the water belches out of the earth, the angel of the water who owns the spring will kill you."

True, Mariano was Chamula—hair tar-black, skin like polished bronze and a grandmother who weaned him on black coffee and diluted *posh*—yet he was a boy. A boy like all other five-year-olds—indecipherable, inquisitive, indefatigable—and he fell! What was worse, he fell by the spring. In that moment the universality of his boyhood ceased and he was instantly a deeply frightened five-year-old Chamula who knew he would become sick and perhaps die.

Mariano trembled with cold fear as he told his grandmother what he had done. With the heel of his small hand he clumsily wiped away salty tears that left irregular streaks on his dirty cheeks. He hoped for some word of reassurance from his grandmother. There was none.

"I warned you never to fall," she said sternly. "Now in a few days you will become sick." And he did. Three days later, Mariano woke with a burning fever, followed with diarrhea and vomiting.

"Your son will die if you don't send for Domingo," said Mariano's grandmother to Miguel. "The owner of the water demands a substitute for Mariano's soul. It is for this reason he has such great sickness."

With a black chicken which had been ceremonially killed and three eggs, Mariano's Uncle Domingo, now acting as the *ilol*, stood beside the spring and begged the owner of the water to accept the chicken and eggs as a substitute for Mariano's soul. "My lord, my holy father, angel and owner of the water," prayed Domingo, "here I come into your presence. Take a look at what I bring you. Now consider that little boy who stumbled and fell in this place. I am begging you to give back the soul of this little boy."

For more than an hour Domingo repeated the same words. Only when he felt that the owner of the spring had heard him did he leave. "Mariano will now get well," he said.

As Mariano grew, so grew his responsibilities. At about age six, the long hours spent hunting birds and sliding down the surrounding eroded banks of his tiny settlement were long-ago memories. Now he spent the long days caring for his family's two dozen scraggly sheep. Though often meat hungry, no Chamula ever ate or sold his sheep. To do so would violate ancient ancestral taboos. Miguel kept his sheep purely for the wool and manure they produced.

Mariano's grandmother often complained to Miguel that the sheep fared better than his own son. "They at least have wool to cover their nakedness," she would complain, "yet the husband of my daughter gives his son who guards the sheep, nothing to cover his nakedness." With a shrug of his small shoulders, Miguel dismissed any reproach for the indifference he felt toward his son.

But it wasn't that simple for Mariano. Each day he lived with the bewildering reality of his parents' disaffection. "No matter what I do," said Mariano to his grandmother one day after his father had belittled him for not holding the machete correctly, "I cannot attain the love of my father. I live now only by hating him."

Because hate is a double-edged sword, Mariano began to hate not only his father, but himself and those around him. To his shame he was nine before he wore his first pair of pants. By age sixteen he had already spent six seasons working from sunrise to sunset picking coffee in the sultry Chiapas lowlands. Only once during that long time did Miguel give Mariano any of the money he had earned. In a rare moment of mock tenderness, he gave his son a couple of pennies to buy some cheap candy. And all the while Mariano's hatred smoldered like hot charcoal under a benign shroud of obedience to his father.

He hated the shopkeepers in Las Casas and *ladinos* because they had things and he had nothing. He hated them because they spoke Spanish and he couldn't. And he hated the *ladinos* who did speak his Chamula language because they, like his father, belittled and treated him with indifference.

His smoldering hatred soon ignited into a swaggering arrogance. His heroes were the strong, dirty fighters and the men who at the president's and council's command, proudly killed dissidents. And like all young men, he dreamed dreams. He wanted what his companions wanted—a little money, a house, and a wife. But for Mariano there was more. He wanted shoes, an expensive pair of pants, and a gun—a pistol!

At night as he lay on his straw sleeping mat, he would dream of a silver barrel pistol with a polished brown handle he had once seen in a store in Las Casas. He would tuck it on the inside of his pants. No one would know he owned one or knew how to shoot it. He could almost feel the cold steel against his flesh. It felt good. A gun would give him confidence to sneer back at the *ladino* who forced him off the sidewalk into a muddy ditch in Las Casas.

If he had a pistol he would just pull it out and wait a moment to see the fear on the *ladino's* face. Then he would leave him dead in the mud. He would do the same to the person who always called him *Mula* (female mule), instead of Chamula. And when the girls all

33

heard how brave he had been they would say, "That is the man I want!"

But it wasn't until he was nineteen that Mariano found the girl *he* wanted.

Chapter

3

HAPPINESS
AND
HEARTBREAK

Happiness and Heartbreak

He saw her first, three days before Ash Wednesday, at the Carnival of Quin Tajimoltic.

Mariano liked this fiesta. It took away the pain of his hard, uneventful life at home and on the coffee plantation. He knew this fiesta, like all fiestas, would end with his father and the fathers of his friends laid out in the weeds or on the damp, dirty ground, drunk, with their wives watching over them. Sometimes the women, with no loss of dignity, also became too drunk to stand and slept off their drunkeness in the weeds beside their husbands.

But before heavy drinking began, there would be the dancers. Mariano always laughed at the men who dressed in dog-like animal skins and paraded through the plaza to the incessantly monotonous rhythm of traditional Chamula music. After the parade, an important person read while selected men reenacted the historic and romantic meeting of Hernan Cortez and the intelligent Mayan woman, Malinche. It was she who became the Spanish conqueror's aide, interpreter, and mistress.

Since women are not allowed to take part in religious festivals, Mariano and the other young men wondered who would play the part of Malinche. The man chosen for this role is kept in isolation for three days before the fiesta and fed a special herb diet. This secret diet is believed to change the man's character and give him feminine ways. After the fiesta, he is given special herbs to return his manhood because the sexual prowess of a Chamula man is all important to him. This, plus verbal dueling—use of obscenities, insults, and inuendo—is important to a Chamula man as well as good-natured fun because it defines his identity. Like the *posh*, it gives him a place of acceptance among his peers.

For this reason, most Chamula girls after age ten are seldom out of the company of a chaperone. A possible exception occurs during the excitement of a fiesta, or when a girl is sent to the water hole or a tiny market store to run an errand for her mother.

And this was where Mariano saw her. He, with several eligible bachelors, stood under the eves of the *cabildo* and watched, first, the parade and hundreds of people who milled through the large plaza. But mostly he and the other young men watched the doorway of a simple store a dozen yards from where they stood.

One of the young men saw her first and with a ribald remark gave Mariano three quick excited jabs in the ribs. "Ah," thought Mariano, "that's the girl I want. Not too skinny, not too fat, long hair to her waist, strong calves and ankles, and her skin . . . ah, her skin is light.''

She was, he thought, the archetype of all Chamula women. And when she came out of the store, without thinking he obeyed an impulse greater than his conditioning. He left the company and security of the bachelor den and walked toward her.

It was wrong. By all Chamula traditions, he knew it was wrong to talk to her where everyone could see. She might already be engaged; she could be beaten for talking to him if someone told her parents. He had to be discreet. Halfway to the store he stopped, and so did she.

It was only for a moment to adjust the carrying strap across her forehead and reposition a 20-liter jug of *posh* on her tiny back, but she looked at him. She didn't smile, nor did she frown. In that inexorable moment their eyes locked and it seemed to Mariano that her eyes glistened.

Slowly, without appearing to be anxious, Mariano followed the girl as she wove her way through the crowd. At one point he passed the clean, whitewashed archway that led into the big church of San Juan Chamula. For an instant he wondered if he shouldn't go inside and pray to San Juan. This was, after all, the fiesta of Quin Tajimoltic, a time for speeches, dances, and a feast of boiled bull's meat for the important people of the community. Yet, more than this it was the time when Chamulas petitioned the Patron Saint San Juan for good crops, material gain, and extra favors. And to make doubly sure they would receive these petitions, special sacrifices and prayers to the earth owner and tribal deities were held in secret caves and on mountaintops surrounding San Juan Chamula.

"Ah," he thought, "if I stop to pray for San Juan to give her to me, I may never see her again. Besides, San Juan never seems to answer my petitions." Having made his decision, Mariano continued to follow her.

As he followed, he noticed she walked toward the narrow canyon where the *mayols* had done their celebrated killing. "If I walk quickly," he thought, "I can get through first and block her way when the trail becomes narrow."

Though barefoot, stooped, and bent under the weight of her heavy load, the girl glided along the pebbly, uneven trail with unusual grace and speed. Intent only on returning to her home, she almost bumped into the waiting Mariano.

"I saw you in the plaza and you looked well to me," he said. "May I carry your load? I am called Mariano."

There were light beads of perspiration across the girl's forehead and bridge of her high classic Mayan nose. She sucked in an extra gulp of air, more from surprise than to fill her lungs. "I am Anita," she said and smiled shyly. For a second time, her soft, dark eyes looked into his. "I live in the settlement of San Antonio. Yes, you may carry my load but only to the edge of my settlement." Her mouth was small and shaped like a miniature scimitar. Her teeth were chalk-white and she laughed easily when he told her how he had followed her.

In the days that followed, Mariano discovered where she grazed her sheep and when she went to the plaza and water hole. And each time Anita saw Mariano she greeted him with a warm smile and they talked when they were sure no one was watching.

She told him how her father had beaten her mother when she was born. "He wanted a son, but when I came out he blamed my mother for her carelessness in having me, a girl." They laughed together knowingly. Each had felt the bewildering pain of rejection. Now for the first time, both found acceptance with someone who understood the tears of loneliness.

There were no words in his vocabulary to describe how he felt. From somewhere deep within his soul, Mariano felt an unexplainable sensation of wanting to give himself away. In a dazzling explosion of first love he saw and felt in Anita all the tenderness he had missed from his mother and father.

"She is like my mother and father all in one person," he said to his bachelor friends one day. But they gibbed him and clung to the old traditions of how, by example, they had been taught to treat a woman. "A woman is for laying with," they said, "for bearing children, cooking, working in the cornfield, and weaving our clothes."

But Mariano saw something his peers did not see—a chance for intimacy. Anita had suddenly made Mariano aware of himself as a person. She was, in his mind, beautiful to look at, beautiful to be with, and he liked what he was when he was with her—alive, complete, and without arrogance. Further, Mariano knew that alone he could not be a true man. He decided to go to his father and ask him to petition Anita's parents for her hand in marriage.

As he walked along the trail toward his hut, Mariano thought about the long series of courtship procedures he would have to follow. The initial step would be to persuade his parents he had made the best choice for a wife. If he succeeded, he would then, since he had no money of his own, ask his father to buy gifts for the bride price.

On the first visit to Anita's parents, Mariano's father, Miguel, or a person chosen to represent him, would take one or two bottles of *posh* and place them at the feet of Anita's father. Kneeling, the petitioner would invite the girl's father to drink the *posh* and in a formal speech, implore him to give his daughter to be Mariano's wife. To buy more time and get more gifts, the parents would refuse and defame Anita's character. She would be accused of being lazy, of not knowing how to weave or grind corn, or worse, of always burning the tortillas. But this was all part of the process and before the petitioner left there was always an arrangement for him to return at a later date.

If, on a fourth or fifth visit, Anita's father accepted and drank the *posh*, a marriage would almost be inevitable. Miguel would then supply six bottles of *posh* and try, through repeated visits and many insults against his son from Anita's parents, to fix a wedding date.

On the chosen day, Miguel would present Anita's parents with 20 liters of *posh*, a kilo of meat, a net of bananas, and a basket of sweet bread and sugar. Insults against Mariano would continue and there would still be a show of bad feelings even if both parties approved the union. Mariano would then eat with Anita's parents for the first time, after which he would serve them *posh* until they were drunk.

On the following day, the bride price gifts would be

divided among Anita's relatives and once again the family would drink themselves into a drunken stupor. Only after all this would Mariano and Anita be considered married.

Mariano stopped just outside the entrance to his settlement and collected his thoughts. Thinking about the possibility of having Anita for his wife made his black-brown eyes smile. And it took away some of the fear he had about approaching his father.

He found his father outside his hut, squatting on his heels, sharpening his machete on a small, flat sandstone. Mariano greeted his father and waited for his response. It was a customary half-audible grunt. His father's indifference and constant belittlement were a never-ending puzzle to Mariano, but he had made up his mind.

"Father," said Mariano respectfully, "I now have nineteen years. I have found the girl I want for my wife."

Miguel didn't look up or slacken his smooth sharpening rhythm. "You may have nineteen years," he said with a sneer, "but you have the head of a goat. You still don't know how to work. You yet cannot sharpen a machete like me. You say you want to take a wife? Ha! What would a woman want with a child?"

"But father," pleaded Mariano, "I like this girl. She likes me. She laughs at the things I say. I feel warm and good beside her. I want to be free to talk to her."

"You have already talked to this girl," said Miguel, "and I don't like it!"

"But there is nothing wrong that I do," said Mariano. "I have no evil intentions."

"I told you before and I tell you now," said Miguel, "I don't want you to talk with this girl. But if you insist and disobey me, you must leave me."

"But Papa," said Mariano holding back the tears, "I have no shoes, I have only one pair of pants, I have no money. I don't want to leave you."

Miguel's voice was hard and unfeeling. "I don't want to see your face anymore. Get out of here and go to another place."

Crushed by his father's words, what self-image Mariano had was stripped away. Without being able to point to the house of his birth and the land of his father, he had no identity or sense of belonging. With pain and shame in his heart, Mariano gathered up his few belongings and hiked to a nearby coffee plantation.

In the weeks that followed, Mariano's focus shifted from the pain of expulsion to the pain of loneliness and the one person who could make it all go away—Anita—and he returned to see her.

"Where have you been?" she asked when he met her by the water hole.

"I have been to the coffee plantation."

"Why did you go there?"

"Because of my father."

"Doesn't your father want you around?"

"No. He and my mother no longer love me. They don't want me."

Anita's eyes glistened and pleaded longingly. "Here I am," she said simply, "you can stay with me. You will be well-off by me."

"Why do you say this? I have no money."

Anita lowered her voice and spoke softly. "Let's just take each other."

"But I have no money."

"But you're a man."

"Yes, what you say is true. I am a man. But I haven't anything in my hands. Everything I should have is in the hands of my father."

"Then work. Earn money."

And Mariano did. Each time he returned from the plantation, Anita greeted him with a smile that was warmly enthusiastic and full of love.

The months passed, Mariano worked hard, saved his money, and thought seriously about marriage. In his mind, Anita was the finest girl in all Chamula. And because he was in love, he wanted to share his feelings with others.

One day he asked the men he worked with how he should act as a husband. "What is it all about? What do I do?" And the men smiled in that way that all men smile who have behaved more like dogs than gentlemen.

"Ha, why marry her?" they said. "Just take her and lay with her now."

"But she is a woman with a straight (righteous) heart," said Mariano. "Her nature is kind and I have not found it in my heart to take advantage of her. We talk and I deeply love her and she me."

"What a stupid goat you are," said the men. "You are a Chamula. You must treat her hard; show her who is boss. Who cares about talk? Be arrogant with her. Tell her she has to lay with you before marriage. And if she is no good, get someone else."

Mariano's face felt hot. The men pointed their fingers and laughed.

But in the days following his conversation with his bachelor friends, Mariano began to think and reflect on their advice. "The men are older and must be right," he reasoned. "Besides, when we talk of marriage she insists I speak with her parents. She wants me to go through the Chamula engagement procedure. I don't want to do this. I have no one to speak for me and I don't want to spend all I have earned on bride price presents."

The longer he thought about what the men had told him, the stronger grew his arrogance. He had always longed for his own identity, something uniquely his which bore the imprint of all the unspoken languages of his soul. And he took this gentle woman and together consumated the most basic of all man's desires.

He was now a man. His peers were right. The best way was to press his advantage. And for a year they shared each other. They talked of marriage. He said *yes*, but only if they eloped. And she said *no*, the right way, the traditional Chamula way, was to ask her mother and father. But Mariano persisted until Anita said, "Yes, I'll do it the way you want. We will just go away together. I will do this because I love you."

They agreed on a time and place to meet—by a large rock on the trail to Las Casas. Then with an exaggerated, self-assured swagger, Mariano told the men he worked with how he had subdued her.

"You are now a real Chamula," they said. "But if you really want to show how strong you are, make her wait more. Be the big boss. Don't go tomorrow."

And Mariano thought the men were right. "I will show her who is boss," he said to himself. "I will show her I can come to her whenever I want."

It was late afternoon on the day after he was to have met Anita that Mariano realized what he had done. His mouth was dry and his breath heavy as he raced toward the rock. There was no one there! "Agh!" he said arrogantly. "Let her go." But it was only a cover, an attempt to deny he had played the fool.

Instinctively he knew she had left Chamula; that he would never again see her. And then like a gushing flood of liquid pain, the feelings came. First into his legs, numbing them. Then into his stomach, deep, deep frustrating pain. Mariano ran into the hills, kicked savagely at a loose stone, and collapsed at the foot of a crusty old pine. The pain continued into his heart. He wanted to scream, his shoulders ached, and he buried his head in his hands and wept.

Chapter

4

HURT,
HATE,
AND HOPE

Hurt, Hate, and Hope

Mariano's heartbreak would stop, but not his fear and hate. As a child he dreaded his father, stood in awe of the healing powers of the *ilol*, and felt sprays of ice-cold panic sweep up his back whenever someone talked about the *brujo* who could change himself into an animal with the power to kill. As he grew older, the fear he felt for his father was overshadowed by the fear he had for the president who could destroy and kill him if he didn't obey Chamula law.

Like a man in a nearby settlement who violated the basic premise of total conformity and threatened the president's security when he put tile on his roof instead of the traditional grass. "You are no longer worthy to live in Chamula," the president had said, and the man was driven from his land.

At nineteen Mariano could not, nor did he want to,

fight the system. For the moment it was less complicated to live without a wife than go through the traditional Chamula engagement procedure. He knew his father would never speak for him and he had no money. Besides, Mariano was afraid of the president and the witchcraft which could be used against him if he forced a girl to marry him. The pain and confusion he felt over losing Anita left him sick at heart and he left to work in the coffee plantations.

With only occasional trips to Las Casas, Mariano spent the next four years picking coffee, drinking heavily, and like most of his male companions, living a life of perpetual ruttishness. There were, however, some positive accomplishments. He learned to speak Spanish, picked up a month of elementary schooling, and understood there was another world beyond the thousand miles of Chamula territory. He also began to hear strange rumors that his uncle and, of all people, his father were somehow linked to a *gringo cashlan*.

"His name is Ken Jacobs," said Mariano's Uncle Domingo one day when Mariano stopped in Las Casas to visit him. "He is a *cashlan*, but his heart is straight."

"What is the work that you do for this outsider?" asked Mariano.

"I work in his garden," said Domingo. "I care for his chickens. He has more than one hundred all in tiny wire cages. He feeds them special food and they all get big and fat. He says he wants to teach Chamulas to have healthy chickens. He tells me chickens get sick when they run free to eat anything."

"Does he speak our language?"

"He speaks our language well, as does his woman."

"What is the work of this *cashlan*?"

"He says he has come to translate God's true words into our language."

"Ah," said Mariano with a turned-down mouth, "I don't understand. I would have no interest in this."

"But you should, Mariano. You should begin to regard seriously the Words of God. It can help you stop drinking the *posh*. And when you don't drink you have more money and live better."

"And my father? What of him?"

"Your father has also regarded seriously God's Word. He no longer drinks the *posh* nor beats your mother."

"Are there others who also seriously regard God's Word?"

"Thirty-five of us come each Sunday to sing hymns and hear your father and me read from the paper called Mark."

"And what of the president and the elders? Do they not consider this new practice an evil against our customs?"

Domingo was silent for a moment. He looked at Mariano with black eyes which came from a bold, craggy face. They showed at once a flicker of fear and determination.

"Son of my brother," said Domingo slowly, "the elders have already decided I should die and so too your father. Rumors in the Las Casas market tell me the elders will hire a killer to do this. But no one knows who it will be or when it will happen."

"If this be so, why have you and my father knowingly disobeyed the rules?"

"I was once an *ilol*," said Domingo. "I followed all

the rules of the elders and our traditions. I drank our *posh* and thought it was holy. I know now it is a curse. I fed the spirits of the dead yet all my religious duties left me empty inside. I felt nothing but hate. If another Chamula's cabbages were bigger than mine, I knew it was because someone had asked the earth owner to curse my crop. And I knew the Chamula whose crop was bigger got that way at my expense, and I hated him like I hated the *cashlan*.

"I hated my wife when she burned the tortillas. I hated her when she wouldn't lay with me. And when she did, I hated her because after it was over I felt just as empty and sick inside. I beat her to try to drive out my hatred, but it never left, and I hated myself because of how I felt.

"But that was my old life. Then I lived as an animal. I got up in the morning believing the sun was my god. I believed witchcraft was my hope and becoming drunk with *posh*, my good health and happiness. Since I have started to obey the Good New Words that Brother Ken is translating into our language, I am different. I now have a new value. I have met a new friend—Jesus Christ who is my helper. I now know I am a son of God. It is for this reason I can no longer follow the rules of our ancestors. My life before wasn't really life at all. And if I am killed, let it be thus. I cannot give up obedience to Christ."

"This is too hard for me to understand," said Mariano. "Besides, I like to drink our holy *posh*. It makes me feel like a strong man, and the women like this."

"You, Mariano, are too Chamula, but you can never live by its system. It will kill you first. The pain you have will never leave unless you regard seriously what God says; unless you ask Him to help you. The proof of your pain is in your own words and actions. You take too many women. You drink too much *posh* only to stop the empty feelings inside.''

Domingo's words puzzled Mariano . . . *new values, a new friend, God's Word, His help, regard seriously* . . . they were empty meaningless words. Yet Mariano did understand what it was to hate. He hated his father for telling him to find his own money and his own wife, and for rejecting Anita when he asked him to speak for her. And he understood pain. For months, his father's words, ''I don't want her for my daughter-in-law,'' had hung in his mind like a bad dream. Yet now, in spite of all the rejection and belittlement, when Domingo said, ''Your father asks for you,'' he felt an obligation to return.

''Perhaps the years away will have softened my father,'' thought Mariano. ''Perhaps he will regard me as a man now that I have my own money, now that I can take a wife.'' But Mariano was wrong. Miguel's response to his son's return was a distant, ''Oh, you are here.''

''Yes,'' answered Mariano, ''I am here.''

''It is good that you have come. There are some things that yet belong to you in my house.''

For several days Mariano carefully observed his father's actions. He saw it was true as Domingo had said. His father no longer beat his mother or drank the *posh*. Along with wondering why his father had asked him to come home, Mariano wondered what strange new force would give his father strength enough to breach the etiquette of this all-important social and religious rite.

It seemed to Mariano an impossible and suicidal resolution and because he didn't want to be censored by the president and elders or knocked down with a lightning bolt by the ancestral gods, he decided to return to the coffee plantations. But in the middle of his deliberations, Mariano attended a funeral and all fear of gods and reprisals was forgotten, and he decided to stay in his father's home.

Except for the immediate family, Chamulas love funerals. They become a mini-fiesta with tortillas, boiled bull's meat, beans, sugar, coffee, and lots and lots of *posh*—all provided free, with great financial strain, by the bereaved family. In this case the only survivor was an old woman. Mariano arrived at dawn in time for the ritual meal and to accompany the procession to the cemetery.

The corpse, an old man who had lived nearby, had been bathed, dressed in clean clothes, and placed in a crude, handmade, pine coffin. In a woven handbag, his widow placed a change of clothes, corn flour, and some nickles in case her husband needed to tip his way into *Vinahel*.

To make sure her husband would get across the great river, the widow put a small bowl of broth containing the head of a chicken in the coffin beside her husband's head. Everyone knew it was the chicken who would guide the dead man's inner soul to *Vinahel*. At the foot of the corpse, the widow placed a gourd of water and some charred tortillas. The soul would need these for the journey.

Yet in spite of these and other preparations for the

sure and safe arrival of her husband's soul into *Vinahel*, the widow clutched her breast and wailed and wept bitter tears. In the background, someone strummed a repetitious three-cord tune on a battered guitar. And on the way to the burial site, still accompanied by wailing and the monotonous guitar music, bleary-eyed friends poured shots-full of *posh* into the dead man's mouth.

The coffin was lowered into a newly dug grave with the corpse's head facing west. When the hole was filled and covered over with fresh pine needles, the widow, in one last pathetic mixture of sobbing and wailing, prayed her last prayer:

> Why, oh why, my son, and you, my husband, did you die? Why, oh why did not god leave you with me? Look how alone and abandoned I am. Left with all the responsibility of feeding (on All Saint's Day) you my dead ones. I have no father, no mother. Oh, my god, oh how could you treat me like this?
>
> Oh my son, oh my husband, bring with you as you come, my father, my mother, and our children. You, my husband, do this for me.
>
> While I live here, while I still have life, the few hours while life endures, it is my hurtful responsibility to wait for you my husband and my children so that I may feed you. Oh why, my god, do you treat me like this?

Mariano had heard all this before. He knew in reality the community cared little for this pathetic, grief-ridden old woman. They were not concerned that she had no one to work her fields or care for her. These who had come were interested only in the free food and *posh*. For a flickering moment Mariano felt a twinge of empathy for the old woman. But it was only a twinge. He, like the others, had come for what he could eat and drink.

Mariano may have reflected longer on the old woman's perplexity had he not suddenly spotted a pretty young girl in the crowd. Suddenly all else was forgotten. He studied her as she walked through the crowd and talked with her friends. Instantly he felt his body awakening to the movements of her body. He ran his tongue over his dry lips. "This is the one for me," he said to himself. "This is the one I am going to have for my wife."

Had he been fully drunk, Mariano may have ruined his opportunity to meet this new passion of his mind. *Posh* always made him feel brave and confident. But he was now more experienced. In his heart he desperately wanted to talk to her immediately. But he knew instinctively this girl had a straight heart and he did not want to spoil her reputation. For once he decided to work within the structure of his society.

It didn't take Mariano long to find out where the girl lived, that her name was Estumina, and that she was a shepherdess. But since she was constantly chaperoned by her younger sisters or mother, it took him four months before he found the right moment to speak with her. And then her only remark was a classic put-down.

Whenever he could, Mariano watched Estumina from a distance, always hoping for a moment when she might be alone, and always deadly afraid some other man might ask for her hand before him. And then it happened. He saw Estumina one day on the trail some distance ahead of her mother, carrying a heavy water jug. Breathing heavy with excitement, Mariano ran down a little hill and met her on the trail.

"I see you carry a heavy load," he said politely. "I will carry it for you."

Without slackening her pace, Estumina clenched her right hand, extended her index finger, and quickly waved it back and forth. "No, no, no!" she said. "I don't think you would be able to."

If a *mayol* had hit him on the head with his oak club, Mariano would not have been more stunned. One well-placed sentence had wounded his pride and put him in his place! Under different circumstances and with a different girl, Mariano may have damned her and told her he didn't want to marry her anyway. But now he smiled inwardly. Intuitively he knew Estumina was worth pursuing. Besides, he thought he caught a tiny glint of favorability in her eye.

"Just you wait," said Mariano to himself. "Just you wait, little Estumina. Some day you're going to be my wife!"

Chapter

5

THE CUTTING HOUR

The Cutting Hour

She was in every way a hag. Her 70-year-old gray hair was matted and snarled. Her feet were bare with leathery, cracked calluses. She walked stooped as if her dirty, goat-smelling, black, homespun, wool garment was a heavy suit of armor. As she picked her way along the trail with the help of a polished, misshapen, oak cane, she seemed like any old Chamula woman who had lived her hard life too long. But those who looked into her face quaked inwardly, gave her wide berth, and hurried past.

It was her cold, searching, sinister eyes that betrayed her. She was a *bruja*, the worst kind of witch doctor. The Chamulas believe and will tell you that in the late dark hours of night, male *brujos* and female *brujas* are seen in cemeteries digging up corpses. Besides living on animal and human blood, everyone knows *brujas* can change themselves into devils which come in all shapes and sizes, some even disguised as hungry jaguars!

Even those who don't believe in devils are sometimes victimized. One day an American painter from New York state traveling through Chamula country, stopped to refresh himself at a Chamula hut. As he sat on a three-legged stool drinking water from a gourd, he began to tease some children by growling like a good-natured bear. The children paled with fear and ran screaming to their mothers. In turn, the women ran to tell their husbands in a nearby field that a large devil attacked the children and was about to change himself into a jaguar.

With phenomenal courage, the men grabbed their single-shot, muzzle-loading shotguns and ceremoniously killed the elderly tourist who thought only to play with these children as he might his own grandchildren.

The men who shot the stranger proudly took his body to the plaza and later to Las Casas. Each thought they would be commended for ridding the Chamula people of such an evil presence. They were, however, arrested and six puzzled men were sent to languish in jail.

The old woman left the market place and tried to avoid suspicion by using a little used trail. But the word was out! Someone had seen her buying candles and they knew she was on her way to the cave. This could mean only one thing. Someone was going to die!

For once, the gossip was true. The old witch doctor *was* on her way to the cave. But what the people didn't know was why, or who had sent her? They would have been surprised to learn she had been commissioned to perform a "cutting hour" ceremony by the president and council of elders.

Word had reached the president of Chamula that a small group of Chamulas met regularly in Domingo's house to sing songs and pray, not to the Patron Saint San Juan, but to the One known as the Holy Cashlan—Jesus Christ.

Meeting in an emergency session, the president reported to the council of elders what he had learned of these Chamulas who were acting in a new and different way.

"I am told some Huixtecos, our so-called cousins from whom we buy our oxen, have believed a new way. They say they believe only in one God, the true God of Heaven. I am told a few of these Huixtecos talked to some of our Chamula men on the trail to Las Casas and have persuaded them to accept this new religion.

"I am also told," continued the president, "these dissident devils who accept this new way, burn the little gods of their houses and no longer drink our holy *posh*. The women of these men like this. They say their men no longer beat them. But how can any man expect his woman to get up early and obey him if he doesn't once in a while beat her?"

The elders smiled and chortled knowingly at this president's wise insight. The president felt the elders' rapport. He was on sure ground and pressed home his point with clenched fist and his finest oratory. "Here you see us brothers of San Juan. We are the elders, the little fathers, sons of our patron saint. It is he who gives power to grow our corn, our beans, our cabbages. It is he who sends the rain and gentle breezes. All of life comes from him and these dissidents no longer regard San Juan. They pray to another.

"If we let these dissidents live, San Juan will be

angry. Our crops will fail! We must never push away our laws and traditions which have come to us from our ancestors. I say death to all of them! We should start with Domingo and Miguel. They are the teachers. The rest we will kill one at a time.''

The president stopped talking. The youngest among them poured the *posh* and each drank in order of their age and rank. The death warrant was signed.

''I will call first for the *bruja*,'' said the president, and each elder nodded his approval.

They walked out of the *cabildo* in single file. They felt good. San Juan would not be offended.

The cave the old witch doctor approached was on the side of a hill which overlooked the central plaza of San Juan Chamula. Its entrance was obscured by several scrub oak and tall brush. To one side of the entrance an old man waited—the *bruja's* husband. Puffing, the old woman clambered up the side of the hill and stopped outside the entrance to the cave. Without a word, her husband lit a pine torch and both walked inside.

About fifty feet into the cave, the pair came to a half dozen small crosses which were stuck into the ground like tilted row markers in a backyard vegetable garden. In front of each cross lay a special clay incense burner. But they didn't stop. Both continued deeper into the recesses of the cave until they passed through a small opening and entered a hall which bristled with elaborate mushroom-shaped stalagmites and stalactites. Here in front of two crosses, one Mayan and the other Latin, the couple stopped, raised their arms with open palms, and mumbled two short prayers.

After praying, the woman, with practiced familiarity,

spread a piece of black cloth on the damp ground. From his carrying bag, the husband drew out a tall bottle of inexpensive *posh*. Next the woman set out two stout candles on a long, narrow board. Beside these, in a clay incense burner, she placed several lumps of charcoal mixed with a few slivers of pitch. She struck a match, and as she lit the resin, a thin stream of smoke rose toward the ceiling of the cave. Satisfied the fire was set, the couple faced the crosses, dropped to their knees, and began a low moaning chant.

> "Holy father! Holy spirit! Father San Manuel! Father San Salvador! Father San Mateo! To you I am appealing."

Then just as suddenly as she started to chant, the old woman stopped and lit the two stubby candles. This was the husband's signal to open the *posh* and serve the first of many drinks, first to his wife and then to himself. For the next quarter hour, the husband and wife witch doctor team moaned a monotone chant, softly at first but rising in volume until both shouted as hard as their voices would allow.

At last as if from a hidden cue, the husband stopped abruptly and pulled out a handful of tiny white candles. Carefully the woman placed them in a neat row on another board—thirty-six in all—the exact number of all known Chamula Christians!

Until this moment, the prayers and chants of the two witch doctors seemed solicitous, even courteous. Now as the old woman lit the tiny candles one by one, the eerie light reflected a new dimension in her eyes—a dimension of hate! With every new candle, the *bruja's* voice rose and fell with anger until the air seemed charged with indescribable malice.

"Holy father! Holy cave! Holy mountain! They are bad, my enemies. They have bad hearts. They are not good . . . ."

She screamed with insane anger as she continued to implore the evil spirits.

"Holy cave, send them the heat of these candles. Give them sickness so they will suffer. Send them disease in blue, in yellow. Send them disease in red, for they are bad! Put in them an animal. Put in them a rat that will devour them slowly and in agony. I have brought you not much, holy spirit. Only the bottle, candles, incense, and pine. We are poor people. Accept our gift. Holy spirit, holy cave, you are great! You are powerful! Hear our prayers."

After her last exhortation, the old woman, in a climactic moment of triumph, grabbed the bottle of *posh* and raised it to her wizened mouth. Her gulps were eager, almost passionate, and she emptied the remaining third bottle of cane liquor as if it were water.

There was one last rite to the "cutting hour" ceremony—the most important. After drinking the *posh*, the old woman tipped the bottle and one by one extinguished the burning candles. By this act she had cut the hour of her enemies—symbolically they were dead. She had killed them. At that moment when all candles had been snuffed out, the old man and woman broke into strange sobs. They were exhausted, emotionally spent, unable to speak.

After a few minutes the couple mumbled the same prayers they had used to begin their macabre incantations, then stopped. It was over and they walked out of the cave to await the inevitable.

For Domingo, Miguel, and the other Christians, the inevitable was immediate pressure and censorship. After flu struck the entire family of a new believer, the father went to a small government clinic to ask for medicines.

"My three-year-old daughter this very day has died from this sickness called flu," said the believer to the clinic supervisor. "I need medicines for my wife and other three children. Especially do I need it for my son. He has but one year and is very sick."

"That is too bad," said the supervisor who knew the man to be a new believer, "but there are no medicines here for Christians."

Later when the new believer told Domingo what had happened, he said, "And when my little son died, those who refused to help laughed gleefully when I laid him into the ground."

In another settlement, the daughter of one of the new believers who herded her sheep with other shepherdesses for protection against coyotes and men, was harassed and forced to herd her sheep alone. The word was out. The president and elders had decreed it—no one was permitted to go near or help her!

Mariano himself would one day become an unwitting casualty of the president's total commitment to discredit and annihilate all believers of this new way. But for the moment no one linked him with the dissident activities which took place in Domingo's house every week. Furthermore, Mariano had no interest in anything his uncle or father were doing. He hardly heard the local gossip or laughter about the lone dissident's daughter who had lost three lambs to coyotes and was fair game for any robust male who wanted to molest her. Mariano's interest was in another shepherdess and how he might arrange to explain his feelings for her.

One day shortly after his first brief encounter with Estumina, Mariano again surprised her on the trail. This time he found a secluded spot behind a large rock which sat on the red clay bank of a gentle creek. Mariano knew Estumina passed by this semi-secluded spot each day to water her flock.

Unaware that Mariano stood hidden behind the rock, Estumina casually herded her slow-moving sheep closer and closer to the creek. When she reached the rock, Mariano suddenly stepped out in front of her.

"Ai, ai!" said Estumina in surprise. "Why are you here?"

Embarrassed and slightly taken back, Mariano banally asked, "Are the stomachs of the sheep filled?"

"Yes," said Estumina with a slight, dimpled smile, "they are filled."

"Good," said Mariano. Then as if he suddenly remembered why he was there, said, "I have watched you. I have seen that you are humble, that your character is strong, and your heart straight. For these reasons, I desire that you will be well-off at my expense. I desire to take you as my wife."

Then in a rare moment of uncommon tenderness, Mariano said, "I don't want to force you, but I am convinced you are in my heart. Because of this, I want it born in your heart that you want me."

"I am willing," said Estumina simply. "But you must first speak to my mother and my father."

Mariano knew this would be Estumina's response and countered with a well thought out reply. "I have looked into your life a little. Your father has many sheep. He is wealthy. And you, Estumina, are valuable to him. Even if we went through all the engagement procedures, it would be in vain. Your father is not ready to give you up to marriage."

"I am sorry, I can't help that," said Estumina. "If you desire me for your wife, you must go through all the traditions of our ancestors. That is the way I want it, and that is the way it will be."

His big, round eyes filled with longing, his mind raced like a runaway mule, and his hands pumped the air for emphasis. "Look," said Mariano, "I have a plan that will bypass all these rules. I can force your father and mother into giving you to me. If you make a commitment to me and want me for your husband, then we will have an affair. After, we will go to the president and authorities and tell them what we have done. Then your mother and father will be called in."

"I don't understand how this will work," said Estumina innocently.

"It will work like this," said Mariano. "In front of the authorities you will say, 'This is the one I want.' The authorities will call your mother and father and when they come, I will say we have laid together and that you want me. In this way we will have violated the engagement pattern. And because your parents haven't given you permission to marry, they will be insulted. The authorities will then say to your father, 'Your daughter has made a commitment to this man. What price do you demand of this man to whom your daughter has committed herself?' ''

It was a devious plan to beat the cultural tradition and would have worked, but it was never put into action. Somehow, Domingo got wind of Mariano's plan and talked him out of it.

"Your father and I are constantly watched for the slightest infraction of Chamula law," said Domingo. "I have heard the elders have assigned a man to kill me. For this reason I no longer work my fields or go into the hills for firewood. My wife must do all these things. Like you, I have worked on the outside and know there is a better way to get the things you want. It will be easier for you just to take Estumina to Las Casas. There you will find a lawyer to make up marriage papers, then like the *cashlan*, you can be married by Civil Law."

Several days later in the late afternoon, Mariano again found Estumina alone and explained this new plan.

"But that would destroy our reputation," she said. "Everyone would know what we had done."

"Yes," said Mariano, "what you say is true. Everyone would know and would talk about us. But don't you want me?"

"Yes," said Estumina, "I do."

"Then let's go," said Mariano. "Let's go right now, this very afternoon. Will you do it for me?"

Estumina hesitated for just a moment, then whispered, "Yes, I will go with you."

Chapter
6

I WANT HER!

I Want Her!

The streets of Las Casas alternate between smooth cobblestones, 18-inch cement tile squares, and rutted dirt with standing pools of muddy water. When the Spaniards erected her in 1528 with conscripted ethnic help (mostly Chamula) and named it after a fair-minded Dominican friar, it became one of Mexico's most enduring towns.

Its buttressed churches, single story dwellings, colonial plaza, and cold, pristine mountain air have shrugged off the passage of over 400 years with casual indifference. In 1965, when Mariano led his bewildered young bride through its crowded, narrow streets, there were a little more than 100 motor vehicles registered in the town's federal building.

Today, when the whole world is infected with the fever of change, Las Casas is beginning to bow under pressure from increased tourist trade, expanding Mexican commerce, and the reality that no one can forever remain isolated in his own cocoon and live. Black-eyed señoritas promenade around the ancient plaza sporting well-tailored pantsuits which replace culturally-accepted skirts and blouses. T.V. antennas jut up from the weather-worn, red tile roofs like upside-down, aluminum garden rakes. And the federal building registers over 1,000 vehicles!

But it is still true that the more things change, the more they remain the same. The emotion and character of Las Casas with all this 20th Century intrusion is still as it always was—a town that exists for the Mayan Tzotzil ethnic peoples. A town which swells by the hundreds of thousands each day with people from ten different Tzotzil dialects—Tzeltal, Chamula, Zanancanteco, Ch'enalo, Huisteco, Mitontic, San Adres, Ixtapa—all these and more. Each with their distinct regional plumage bring to the streets and markets of Las Casas an unequaled riot of color and excitement.

Yet just as the town swells each dawn with ethnic peoples to buy and sell, so it deflates at sunset. When the last accordion-type, metal shutter rattles down in front of a glass show window and the final bolt slides behind a heavy, wooden, shopkeepers door, it's as if that very act causes the last remaining ethnic person to vanish into the cold night air.

It was for this reason, that late December night in 1965, that Mariano and Estumina became an instant curiosity to the late night shoppers and merchants closing down their businesses. While Estumina didn't understand their Spanish vulgarities and suggestive remarks, she could feel their intent and was uneasy. But then she had been uncomfortable ever since she had arrived three days before. The large, bustling crowds, hawkers, and cold, unfamiliar, and indifferent surroundings completely disoriented her. And her marriage "ceremony" that afternoon only added to her discomfort and bewilderment.

Following Domingo's advice, Mariano located a lawyer who made up the long, complicated marriage contract. In a small, second-story office just off the plaza, Estumina had stood stone silent, ramrod straight, tightly holding Mariano's elbow as the lawyer asked their ages.

"I think I have 25 years," said Mariano.

"And the girl," asked the lawyer, "how many years does she have?"

"I think she has 19."

"Really?" said the lawyer quizzically.

"Yes," said Mariano, "just look at her."

The lawyer did. And Estumina could feel the heat of his look. She perspired nervously and resented being humiliated by the hated *cashlan*.

Two days later, Estumina stood before the judge with the same feelings of discomfort and nervousness. By prearranged plan, she was to say "Sí" to the Spanish-speaking judge every time Mariano poked her. Later, Mariano explained that the judge had asked her if she promised to be a good, dutiful and faithful wife and did she accept him as her husband.

Mariano also explained that now they had the documentation to prove they were legally husband and wife and the Chamula authorities would have to accept them as being married.

Mariano was happy; he had beat the system. But not

Estumina. Inwardly she was homesick and resentful that Mariano had talked her out of a traditional Chamula wedding—a wedding which would have involved her family; where they could have eaten and drunk together. Also, there would have been a charge by the elders of the clan to Mariano that he should buy her new clothes once every two years. But now there was no promise and no obligations.

"And where now, my new husband, are you taking me?" asked Estumina after the ceremony was over.

"Domingo works and lives in the big yard of the *gringo cashlan*," said Mariano. "He told me he has room. There are some clean, unused, brick chicken pens we can live in for a few days before we go back to my father's house."

Mariano did the traditional thing by returning to live for a time in his father's house but did the non-traditional thing by not presenting himself to his new father-in-law. After three months when he needed money, Mariano acted within the cultural patterns. He left his new wife with his mother and sisters and went to work in the coffee plantations.

His action was normal but the consequences which resulted from his decision became one of Mariano's most serious errors in judgment.

"I leave one-hearted," said Mariano to Estumina when he left her. "You will be well-off in my mother's house."

But Estumina wasn't. Almost as soon as Mariano left she became a Cinderella in her mother-in-law's house. No matter how hard she tried, Estumina could never grind the corn fast enough, make the corn dough correctly, or pat out the tortillas to the desired thickness. Commands given by her mother-in-law were counter-commanded by the sisters-in-law. And at night when she curled up in her dank corner to sleep with her face to the mud wall, the family snickered as Estumina tried to stifle her sobbing.

Finally, after two months of unbearable loneliness and oppressive belittlement, Estumina announced she was returning to her father's house.

"Here I have come," said Estumina when she returned. "I have done what I have done. If you are willing to have me with you in the house, I will stay here."

"It is good that you have come to visit us, little daughter," said Estumina's mother, "but your rightful place and the place you belong is with your husband's mother and sisters."

"But, little mother," pleaded Estumina, "I am not one-hearted there. I feel no love from his mother or sisters. They only use me to do all their work and laugh at me when I don't understand what they have told me to do. I wish to stay here with you."

With his leather carrying bag heavy with three month's wages, Mariano returned completely confident that Estumina would be at his mother's house, happy and eagerly awaiting his return.

As he had often done in the past, Mariano stopped first to visit Domingo who was now working full-time helping Ken Jacobs translate the New Testament scriptures into the Chamula language. Since Domingo served both as grounds' keeper for the enclosed acre property and translation helper, it was he who opened the narrow, metal door when Mariano rang the bell.

"It is good that you have come, son of my brother," said Domingo, "because I have news that concerns you. Your wife no longer lives at the house of your mother. She lives again with her own mother and father."

"How can this be?" said Mariano anxiously. "Have I lost her?"

"I do not know," said Domingo, "but I suggest you investigate the reasons she now lives in this other place."

After a hurried cup of thick, black coffee which he drank from Domingo's chipped, blue enamel mug, Mariano left for San Juan Chamula on the back of a pickup crammed with bleating goats. The trip was cold and dusty but he didn't care. He thought only of Estumina and what it was that could have caused her to go back to her family.

When he reached the brow of a little hill which overlooked the house of his father-in-law, Mariano was both frightened and angry. Since he had eloped with Estumina and never formally asked her father for her, he had no right to talk with Estumina's parents. Furthermore, if he did, her father might beat him.

Cupping his hands around his mouth, Mariano puckered his lips and blew a long, shrill whistle. It was the same secret whistle he had used many times to call Estumina to him when they were courting and didn't want her parents to know he was hiding in the woods. Estumina had almost always answered immediately with a whistle of her own. Now the only thing Mariano heard was the sound of a cool breeze sweeping through the ponderosa pines. Mariano whistled a second time. Still no answer. "Ah, she doesn't want me," he thought.

"She's there. She hears my whistle, but doesn't answer."

As with Anita, Mariano believed he had found in Estumina the antidote for all his loneliness and rejection. Now again the confusion and pain crushed his soul and deadened what he thought was the seed to his true identity. The woods were there and he again retreated into the coolness of its womb to find solace and comfort.

But this time it was different. Instead of weeping, although he felt like it, he was filled with anger and hatred. Hatred against the whole Chamula system, against all those who had more than he did, against the way he had to live, cheat and contrive to find a few moments of happiness and peace. When he thought he possessed it, he discovered it was only an elusive dream and he swore out loud. "*Cabrónes!* Sons of he-goats! I'll make them pay for this!"

"I am sorry your wife has left your house," said the lawyer who had drawn up Mariano's marriage papers. "But what is it that you want of me? Do you want to divorce her?"

"No, no!" said Mariano. "I don't want to get rid of her. I want her! What I want is to discover if the parents of my wife forced her to abandon my house. I am told there is a paper you can send that will bring my wife and her parents before the authorities to inquire about this."

"Yes," said the lawyer, "under Mexican law you can send her parents a subpoena. They will then have to appear before the District Attorney in Las Casas or before the president and elders of Chamula, whichever place you wish."

"I wish it to be before the authorities in Chamula," said Mariano.

"Then," said the lawyer, "it will be as you requested."

Mariano came apprehensively to the *presidencia*, a newly built building for conducting tribal affairs. He doffed his palm woven hat and stood respectfully just outside the president's door. "Are you here, my older brother?" called Mariano.

"I am here, younger brother," said the president. "What help can I be to you?"

Carefully Mariano explained how much he wanted Estumina and how disappointed he was when he didn't find her waiting in his father's house.

"Please," said Mariano, "I beg of you to help me."

"Are you truly married?" asked the president.

"Yes," said Mariano. "I have papers to show this."

"Then, younger brother, do not worry. It can be arranged."

With his hands cupped over his silver-knobbed staff, the president turned to a waiting *mayol*, raised his thick eyebrows, and said, "Bring in Estumina and her parents immediately."

In that mysterious way known only to those who live in a closed community, the word was out before the *mayol* left that exciting things were happening at the *presidencia*. And it was the crowd who announced by their muttering that Estumina and her parents had arrived.

With only a cursory nod to the president, Estumina's father spoke directly to Mariano. "What is it you want?" he demanded.

"I want nothing from *you*," said Mariano. "I want

only what is by your side.''

Estumina's father turned and pointed with his chin to Estumina who stood silent beside him. ''You are not going to have her!'' he said with a sneer. ''There was not a thing that I ate from you.''

Here it was again—tradition—the bride price he never paid. The battle was more than just the legal right to reclaim his wife. It was a battle against the whole Chamula marriage pattern and Mariano winced.

The president spoke before Mariano could answer. ''Your words are hard. This man and your daughter are legally married.''

''That does not matter,'' said Estumina's father. ''I will be responsible for all expenses that are required to divide them.''

''Have you asked your daughter if this is her choice?'' asked the president.

''She doesn't want the man!'' said Estumina's father.

''But Estumina is not speaking for herself. Let us see if this is really her choice,'' said the president.

Turning to Estumina, the president, with a touch of uncommon courtesy, smiled and asked her gently if she wanted Mariano for her husband. There was no answer. ''Open your mouth and speak to us!'' said the president firmly. ''Let us know your heart.'' But Estumina lowered her head and stared blankly at the clay floor.

''You see! You see!'' said Estumina's father excitedly. ''She doesn't want this man.''

''She doesn't speak because you have commanded her not to speak,'' thought Mariano. He wanted to tell the president this but out of respect said nothing.

Repeatedly the president addressed Estumina and

asked her to speak. When kindness failed, he turned to ridicule and sarcasm and called her a little girl.

"It is obvious my daughter does not want this man," said Estumina's father.

"It still does not come out of her mouth that she doesn't want him," said the president. "You are the only one who says this."

For the remainder of the day the president, while attending to other business, tried in vain to make Estumina answer him. Finally Estumina's father, after repeatedly stating that Estumina didn't want Mariano for a husband, asked how much it would cost to have them separated.

"You don't have enough to pay," said the president out of the corner of his mouth.

With a look of triumph on his heavy face, Estumina's father drew out a cloth bag from under his *chamarra* and plunked it down on the pine wood table. "Here," he said. "One thousand pesos in silver coins!"

Outside the *presidencia* the crowd stood in expectant silence as if watching a scene from a great play. The president rubbed his course hand over his chin for several moments. Then as if it were for the first time, looked at Estumina's father and asked, "Do you desire for them to be separated?"

"That's what I want," said Estumina's father.

"And you, Estumina," said the president as he turned to look at her, "is this what you want?" As if she were set on a predetermined course, Estumina said nothing.

"All right," said the president as he picked up the bag of money, "if this is what you want, then this is the way it will be."

Chapter
7

LET IT BE THUS

Let It Be Thus

Mariano folded his arms under his white *chamarra* and made his way across the almost deserted central plaza of San Juan Chamula. It was cold, and a fine mist hung in the predawn air like suspended steam. He shivered as he walked toward the *cabildo* but he knew it wasn't the dank humidity that made his teeth chatter. It was his fear of losing Estumina. For three days the president and elders had unsuccessfully tried to persuade Estumina's father to change his mind.

From the beginning of the negotiations, the president seemed anxious to help Mariano. Repeatedly he told him not to worry. But the heavy thunk of hard cash and each day's impasse clearly worried Mariano.

At the end of the second day, Mariano had stayed behind to ask the president what he could do now that Estumina's father had given money.

"Does Estumina still remain in your heart?" the president had asked. When Mariano assured him that she did, the president had said, "Good! I see your heart to be straight, younger brother. It is that *cabrón* of a man who insists on keeping his daughter for himself who has the fault. Don't worry. Estumina is still your gift. Tomorrow we will deal harshly with him."

Mariano had returned to his quarters confident Estumina would warm his blanket the following night. But the battle which had begun with the winds blowing in his favor, shifted once again by evening.

"You know very well your daughter and this man agreed to marry," the president had said to Estumina's father. "Why do you hinder their hearts in fulfilling their desires?"

Blind with rage, Estumina's father had countered every logical plea with, "My daughter no longer wants him."

Finally, late in the afternoon of the third day, Estumina's father had said, "I paid one thousand pesos. What more do you want?"

"So be it," the president had said. "If divorce is what you want, then divorce is what it will be. But it is late now. Let us all return to the *cabildo* early tomorrow. Then I will have all the documentation ready to sign."

"Older brother," said Mariano as he entered the *cabildo*, "this is now the fourth day. Estumina has not yet spoken one word and I fear her father will take her back."

"Younger brother," said the president, "don't worry. There are lots of other girls to warm your blanket but I believe you will not have to take another. This very night Estumina will be by your side. Now before Estumina and her father come, let me explain my plan . . . ."

Estumina entered the *cabildo* as she had done each morning—a few steps behind her father, eyes downcast and locked into an unseen object on the floor. Her father had revealed nothing but contempt for Mariano and this morning his haughty swagger showed he anticipated imminent victory and revenge.

Flanked by his elders, the president opened the fourth day of negotiations by again telling Estumina's father he thought it would be better for him if Mariano and Estumina stayed together.

"Look, brother, how much it is hurting you. One thousand pesos is a great sum of money."

"That is the way I want it," said Estumina's father.

"Very well," said the president. "Here then are the papers for you to sign."

A *mayol* passed the papers to Estumina's father with copies to Estumina and Mariano. At this point, Mariano began to put into action the president's plan. "What am I to do?" he asked.

"If you want a divorce from Estumina, then sign your name to the paper," said the president.

"But I am not asking for a divorce," said Mariano. "It is Estumina's father who wants us to separate. Therefore, I will not sign."

"Then what is it that will make you sign? Will money?" asked the president.

As prearranged, Mariano ran his fingers through his thick black hair. "If I were to separate, how much money would come to me?"

Immediately Mariano felt someone tug his sleeve. In a low whisper an older man cautioned him. "Be careful, younger brother. It is not good that you take money. Estumina's father could pay the *bruja* to curse you. You then would get sick and die. Let her go without money."

Neither Mariano or the president had considered this. Mariano felt a twinge of cold fear and began to wonder if they should continue with their scheme to ask for money. He had to think fast! The president was speaking to him.

"What is on your mind, younger brother? How much would you demand of Estumina's father?"

Without stopping to think further of the consequences, Mariano replied, "Let him pay me $600.00 pesos."

So that all would know he was honest and wise in his dealings, the president recapped the details of the divorce negotiations.

"You, the father of Estumina, have paid to me, the president and elders, $1,000.00 pesos. Is that true?"

"Yes, it is true," said Estumina's father.

"Now will you pay to Mariano $600.00 pesos? Do you possess it?"

"I have it."

"Then pay Mariano."

As before, Estumina's father pulled out a cloth bag from under his *chamarra* and clunked down $600.00 silver pesos. As Mariano picked up the bag to stuff it into his own carrying bag, the president had his cue. Immediately he began to criticize him.

"Younger brother, you have made a mistake. You have asked for too little money."

"I don't understand, esteemed older brother," said Mariano. "Why have I made a mistake?"

"The mistake is this, younger brother. If you want a divorce which says you can be immediately free to marry another woman, you will have to pay me $600.00 pesos. If you don't want to pay or don't want another partner, then this divorce will take three months or maybe longer."

"How much longer?" asked Mariano.

"As long as two or three years!"

"But, president," pleaded Mariano, "why should I have to pay when I am not the one asking for a divorce? Don't you see it is Estumina's father who should pay? He has the fault. It is he who wants to take away what is really under my hands and feet (under my control). I already have $600.00 and this is mine. If he wants Estumina to be free to go immediately to another man, let him pay the extra $600.00. I cannot!"

"Such big words from a little man," said Estumina's father. "I have given the president $1,000.00 and another $600.00 pesos to you, and now you demand yet another $600.00 pesos for the president. Where do I find it?"

"That is not my problem," said Mariano.

Without bowing to the president or asking permission to leave, Estumina's father turned and stalked out of the *cabildo*. Believing he had gone to borrow the extra $600.00 pesos, Mariano turned to the president and asked permission to speak with Estumina. The president smiled and nodded.

"Why is it in all these days there has not one single word come from your mouth?"

Estumina heard Mariano but, as before, was silent.

"Why is it, woman, that I see you like a tree that cannot speak?"

For the first time in four days and since he had left for the coffee plantations, Estumina looked into Mariano's face and spoke to him. "It is you that has the sin," she said coolly.

"Me? Me?" said Mariano incredulously. "How is it that I have the sin?"

"Look to yourself," said Estumina defensively. "It was you who never came to my house to look for me."

"But I did come," said Mariano. "I came immediately from the plantations and whistled for you. It was you who didn't answer me."

"I never heard you," said Estumina. "But that no longer matters. Look at all the money you have taken."

"Is not that the way you wanted it?"

Mariano urged Estumina to continue talking, but as if she had been programmed for only these few words, she stopped and continued her vigil of silence.

When it appeared Estumina's father would not return with the extra money, the president called Mariano and Estumina to stand together.

"Younger brother, it appears your father-in-law will not return. I, therefore, declare an end to this whole affair. Woman, here is your husband. Younger brother, here is your wife. Go with each other."

"Let us go," said Mariano as he took Estumina by the hand.

"Let it be thus," said Estumina and together they walked out of the *cabildo*. Mariano was $600.00 pesos richer and had defeated his powerful father-in-law. But what was more incredible, he had his wife to warm his blanket. It was truly a day to celebrate and they headed for the cantina.

Shortly after the two young people left, Estumina's father returned to the *cabildo* and told the president he was unable to raise the money. "Do not worry, brother," said the president. "Before your very eyes let it be known that your daughter and Mariano are taking each other. This is the end of it!"

This, however, was not the end, but the beginning. The beginning of a long, hard chain of events which would turn Mariano and Estumina's world upside down. The odyssey began with a drinking bout which loosened Estumina's tongue and returned Mariano and Estumina to his father's house, too drunk to stand.

"You only are mine," said Mariano to Estumina amorously after his first four shot-glasses of *posh*. Is it true that you really love me?"

"Yes," said Estumina, "I love you."

"Then let us drink on it and open your heart to me and tell me why you did not speak a word in all those days."

"I was afraid," said Estumina. "When I lived in your father's house I felt pushed aside by your mother and sisters. I wanted you but I thought I could not stand to suffer again under your mother's hand."

"But look at the suffering you put your father through," said Mariano. "Now there is a great gap between your father and me. It will take many years before he will speak to me. How much better things would have been if you had opened your mouth. Was it your father who commanded you to be silent?"

"No," said Estumina, "I remained silent because I wanted to for the reasons I have already said."

"But your father must have commanded you to be silent."

"No, it was my own decision."

"Then there is nothing more we can do but forget it and love each other," said Mariano.

"Let it be thus," said Estumina as she gulped down her tenth glass of *posh*.

But deep inside Mariano knew it would not *be thus*. As the cane liquor freed Estumina's inhibitions, she alternated between tears and guilt-filled babblings about "how could she forgive him when he had damaged her parents so."

The day ended as the president had predicted, with Estumina by Mariano's side, but not as Mariano had hoped it would be. Both had to be dragged to his father's house and were dumped onto the floor to sleep off what Mariano had called, "a celebration to wipe out the anger in our hearts toward each other."

It had been light for a long time when Mariano awoke. He yawned. His mouth felt as if it were filled with straw.

"I see you greet the day sadly," said Mariano's father. "It is good you are awake because I have something for you to consider."

"Go ahead and tell me," said Mariano.

"Consider this, my son. I do not want you and your wife around my house. I have come to believe the Good New Words. I have also come to see that you and your wife are hard drinkers and I don't want devils in my house. If you want to obey and believe the Good New Words, you can both live with us. On the other hand, if you don't want to believe and obey—get going!"

Mariano's head felt like a split cabbage but he

understood the implications of what his father had said. He knew he didn't have enough money to buy his own land and house, and as he had done so many times before, submitted to his father's authority. Outwardly he conformed, but inwardly he hated himself and cursed the circumstances which forced him to act contrary to his own judgment.

He ran his thick tongue across his furry front teeth. "I will give up drinking," he said lamely.

"Good," said his father. "In a few days I will leave for Las Casas to be at the house of Brother Ken. In the meantime, you should attend the meetings of the new believers. On Sunday they all meet in the house of Domingo. It would be good for you to learn about the Good New Words."

But Mariano was not interested in this so-called Good New Words. He had heard the same words from Domingo—that if he obeyed the teachings of God and His Son, Jesus Christ, he could be set free from the power of sin in his life. But how could he obey all the laws of God when he couldn't obey all the laws of the elders? Yet Domingo had told him Jesus could give power to stop drinking and would become his Helper if he accepted His offer of love. And at this moment he needed all the help he could get if he wanted to live in his father's house.

This concept of Jesus becoming one's own personal Helper had captured the minds and hearts of many Chamulas and infuriated the president and elders. One of these was a vivacious 18-year-old Chamula woman named Paxcu. (Both of her parents had been killed a few years earlier in a drunken argument about whom she should wed. She now had the full responsibility for her brother, a younger sister, and sometimes the children of another sister.)

The local grapevine had it that the wife of the *gringo cashlan* knew how to cure sickness faster and better than the *ilol*. Paxcu didn't know if this was true or not, but decided to find out for herself and rang the bell of the metal door on Avenida Jose Maria Santiago in Las Casas.

"I have come for medicines to cure the pain in my stomach," said Paxcu to Domingo when he opened the door.

"The *cashlans* are not here," said Domingo. "They are in the country and house where they were born. But the *señora* has taught me what medicines to give for the pain you have."

Since worm infestation affects most Chamulas, the first order of any treatment is anti-worm medicine. In Paxcu's case, the results were so dramatic she returned to her settlement unable to keep silent about the wonderful new medicines that worked better than witchcraft.

By nature, Paxcu was interested and curious about all things new and was fascinated with the story of Jesus and His love for her. Each Sunday for four weeks she returned to sit in the front row of the little Bible study service Domingo held. And each week Paxcu became more talkative until someone reported her to the president and she was almost never to talk again.

A new president had just been installed and he with his new staff decided once and for all to make an example of this defenseless girl. "It is time we killed all those who are interested in this new way which is contrary to the traditions of our ancestors," they said.

About midnight on the Thursday of the fifth week

she attended Domingo's Sunday services, a dozen Chamula men, fully armed, walked silently toward Paxcu's small thatch-roof hut. In Chamula fashion, Paxcu slept naked with her heavy wool skirt as her blanket. In the hut with her was her 12-year-old brother, 13-year-old sister, and two nieces—Angelina, four, and Abelina, five, who were asleep in a crude crib.

Without a word, Xalic, the leader of the band, pointed to the gasoline can one of the men carried and motioned to the roof. He then cocked his single-shot shotgun and positioned himself squarely in front of the small, wooden, plank door. Behind him the remainder of the band stood ready. Moonlight glinted off their machetes.

As the heavy acid smoke began to swirl around Paxcu's head, she started to cough. It took her only a split second to rouse herself and scream to the other children to get up.

She reached the door in a single bound and flung it open. To her horror, Xalic blocked her escape. With a sinister sneer on his lined face, he aimed his gun point-blank and shot. Twenty-one lead pellets tore into Paxcu's attractive face and neck and she slumped in the doorway.

Though her body was stunned, the mechanism of Paxcu's energetic mind drove her to immediately get up. Instinctively she knew the long knives would be next. Like a frightened deer, Paxcu sprang into the bright moonlit night and was immediately grabbed by Xalic's outstretched arm.

As she would tell the story later, Paxcu said, "It was because I was naked. I just wriggled out of his grasp and flew into the cornfield. With God's help I found the house of my uncle and survived.''

Paxcu survived, but in the morning the outside authorities, attracted by the fire, found the charred remains of her 13-year-old sister. A nearby chicken coop yielded the severely wounded, blood-splattered forms of her two nieces. Angelina died on the way to the hospital. Only Paxcu's brother and five-year-old Abelina lived. To this day, Abelina carries the heavy diagonal imprint of Xalic's machete across her full lips.

Months later at a police-type lineup, little Abelina courageously looked into the hard face of her assailant and said, ''You are the one who killed me when I was standing in my little bed.''

Before this, however, news of the killings and house burning became a fiery cross against all known believers. In more than a dozen settlements, believers had their pigs shot, houses burned, and crops destroyed. At night, many believers fled into the cold surrounding hills and slept in caves or in the forest. They could never be sure when an attack like the one against Paxcu would occur.

Since Mariano's father, Miguel, and Domingo were the known leaders, they and all who lived in their houses were marked for the next wave of persecution.

Chapter
8

THE HELPER

The Helper

This was not the first time a president had harassed the new believers and forced them to take refuge in the hills or Ken Jacob's yard. There had been earlier incidents several years before when a small group of believers from another area was ambushed and shot while going to Sunday services in a nearby chapel. Two died and the believers had appealed to the governor of the state to protect them. But who could protect and be concerned for such a tiny minority? And who could control a Chamula when he was drunk at fiesta time which was the time of greatest danger for most of the believers?

There was also the time when Domingo had just finished supper and his barking dogs announced the arrival of a large group of men. "Throw ashes on the fire!" he ordered. "Everyone lay flat on the ground!"

Domingo only had time to bolt his heavy, wooden door and fling himself on the floor beside the others before the holocaust broke loose. For two hours, a hundred men poured volley after volley into the house. Domingo's wife complained she almost went deaf with the noise.

The only one hurt during the shooting was Domingo's nine-year-old daughter, Chati. At one point she raised her head above the 18-inch rock foundation and a bullet tore through her cheek knocking out her tooth. "Mommy," she screamed, "I have a bullet in my mouth," then promptly spit out tooth and bullet.

After the shooting at Domingo's, the president warned all followers of this "new way" that this was only the beginning of what would happen if they continued contrary to the accepted Chamula traditions. Some believers were frightened and turned back to the old ways. Others continued steadfast, encouraged by reports of God's protection.

Miguel was quick to relate an incident which happened after he and Domingo had spent several days in the hills fasting and praying for God's protection of "these new in the faith." After his prayer session, Miguel met a man in the Las Casas market and began sharing the Good New Words with him. "It is interesting you should tell me this Gospel is good and can help me stop drinking," said the man, "because on the last Day of the Dead I was one of many men going to kill you and Domingo. We had all drunk the *posh* but a strange happening stopped us. When we came near your house, a fear came into us so that some of the bravest among us trembled. No one dared go any closer. We only looked into the darkness of your house.

"Finally we decided not to try and kill you but get your brother-in-law Domingo. But as we came near to his house an even greater fear came upon us. Two of the men forced themselves to within shouting distance of Domingo's house but when no one answered, they quickly joined us and we left."

Miguel also liked to tell how on another occasion while his wife was alone in the house, she heard a group of men outside waiting for him. "When she realized they meant me harm, she began to perspire heavily. Then she knelt down and began to pray. She knew I was to come back soon and wondered how she could warn me. Suddenly she saw the light of my flashlight touch the eaves of the house and screamed a warning.

"When I heard her yell, I grabbed a big stick and ran yelling, 'I come in the name of the Lord!' When the killers heard this, they all fled into the night."

There was also the time Miguel dressed up as an old woman and outwitted a group of killers who had pursued him six days through the forest.

While Miguel and Domingo were courageous believers, they were also babes in understanding many aspects of what it meant to know and follow God's ways. Miguel especially needed instruction in Christ's command to "love one another" in his relationship toward Mariano and Estumina. Yet during times of persecution, it was stories like these and others that gave the small band of believers courage to continue meeting and sharing their faith. But this new harassment was different.

This time the president had a general—Xalic, who while hated by many Chamulas for collecting heavy taxes, was nonetheless a powerful and outspoken antagonist of all Christians. It was he who had organized and carried out the attack against Paxcu. Now under his direction he mobilized a great number of Chamula men to watch and block the main trails to and from San Juan Chamula. Each man was given orders to kill anyone known to be a follower of the new way. Since those who fled the persecution could not return to their homes, they turned to the only person they knew would help them—Brother Ken, the *cashlan* who was translating God's Word for them.

After the believers had been in their yard for several days, Ken and Elaine Jacobs wrote the following letter:

The strong winds of persecution are blowing hard upon the little band of Chamula Christians. They are being "sifted as wheat." All the Christians, except one wife and one feeble old lady, are here in our yard. The place seems like Grand Central Station. Not one of them dare go back into Chamula territory lest they be ambushed on the trails or murdered in their homes. They have abandoned their houses, corn crops, chickens, turkeys and whatever earthly possessions they had. We have loaned them blankets and floor space. Where they don't fit they look around our yard for other places to sleep. Last night three men slept in our baggage trailer. One family slept on top of the corn crib. I noticed three young girls sleeping in the wheat bin.

Both Domingo and Miguel's homes were fired on by a hundred or more men. Domingo's family, wife, old grandma, and four children were miraculously spared by pressing their bodies against the dirt floor as the bullets ripped over them. A runner warned Miguel's family and they fled into the hills before the killers got close.

Domingo's neighbors have taken over his property and he expects them to appropriate his land. The old grandma was able to sneak back to the house and bring out Domingo's five chickens. After three hours on the trail, she arrived at our place and pulled them out of the sack. Only three lived. Domingo's family wept as they saw this. It represented a loss of three week's savings.

Their enemies laugh and vow if they return, not a man, woman, or child will be left alive. Trails are blocked and watched as hundreds with guns and machetes are committed to carry out the tribal elders' orders. Mexican authorities, though sympathetic, seem helpless to stop the wild mob action of those against the Christians.

Last night we got together to sing some hymns and I read the translated portion of Mark 10:28-31, " . . . Lo we have left everything to follow you . . . . " You should have heard them talk and compare themselves to Jesus' followers. When I suggested we break up and get some sleep, one Chamula man said, "Let's sing some more and hear more of God's Word!"

The other night, about 2:00 a.m., some of the Chamula Christians slipped back into Chamula territory to try and rescue some of their food and blankets. They found their homes slashed by machetes and doors ripped off. The barking of dogs warned them of the approaching enemy and they fled into the hills. The old grandma, tired and cold, threw herself against the wall of one of the houses and said, "If they kill me, they kill me, but I can't make it back to Brother Ken's house." The cold, tired band came back about 6:00 a.m. without the old grandma and one man's wife. They were not able to rescue anything! Elaine made some hot coffee and toast for the young women while others made fires in our yard to cook their food and warm themselves.

While there are hot tears of grief among the believers, we haven't heard a single person say they would give up following Christ. I do hear them saying, however, that in the next few days every one of their homes will be burned to the ground.

Yesterday the group quietly gathered around while Elaine and I played a Chamula hymn on a little phonograph. As the record played, I noticed a young woman pull her shawl over her head and sob until the music stopped.

Our eyes are upon Him alone Who called us to this task of translating God's Word for them, though at times it seems so hurtful.

Like refugees from any war, the Chamula Christians had to be resettled in homes of their own and into the community. While Ken Jacobs used his many personal contacts to locate temporary housing for the displaced Chamulas, state and federal authorities tried to convince the Chamula elders of the believers' constitutional rights.

At first the elders, in a fanatical desire to preserve Chamula tradition, refused to acknowledge any law but Chamula law and renewed their vows to kill all

Christians who returned. In the past, local and federal government had treated Chamula territory almost as a sovereign state. The only official contact was an assigned government agent to act as an intermediary. Few local government agents wanted to become directly involved with the hard-drinking, volatile Chamulas. Now because of its far-reaching implications against the Mexican constitution, the federal authorities were demanding that Chamulas aid and protect those being driven from their homes.

But the elders refused and doubled their intensity against the Christians. Their orders, contrary to the Mexican authorities' demands, were that no one speak to or protect a known Christian. Those that did would violate tribal traditions and like the Christians, would be killed.

Then three months to the day after the persecution began, the elders, in a surprise move, agreed to a limited protection for the Christians if they returned. The official statement said, ''We can grant protection to the Christians only during the day (who can protect a person at night?) and only if they live near the political and religious centers of Chamula.''

To test their statement, some of the women returned first. The believers knew women are seldom killed without their men. Later, when nothing happened, their men returned to thicken and fortify the mud walls of their houses and repair the ripped, burned-off doors. But at night, to escape a surprise attack, those who returned slept in the surrounding hills, forests and caves.

For a while there appeared to be a facade of peace. But because they were unsure of the elders' intentions to keep their word, many Christians lived part-time in Chamula to work their gardens and part-time in Las Casas.

For many months, rumors in the Las Casas market had it that the elders had hired killers to get Domingo. The current rumor was that the "peace treaty" was only a ruse to lure Domingo, and now Miguel, back into the tribe together. Ever since the very first disturbances, Domingo and Miguel had frustrated the elders by going in and out of Chamula secretly and separately.

In the meantime, the struggling band of Christian Chamulas was being ministered to by believers from other ethnic groups. Nicolas, a small, mild-mannered believer from the adjoining Huixteco people—who himself had felt the hot fires of religious persecution— walked five hard hours to bring encouragement from the Beatitudes in Matthew, chapter five. And through it all, Mariano and Estumina cursed themselves for being in the wrong place at the wrong time. They were numbered with the believers and forced to think seriously about becoming true followers of Jesus Christ.

Before he could give himself to a serious spiritual reconciliation and consideration of what it meant to allow Jesus to become his Helper, Mariano had to reconcile his own domestic affairs.

"Man," said Estumina one day, "don't you think it would be good to have a place of our own?"

"We need to wait," said Mariano.

"Ever since we fled to live in Señor Jacobs' yard, we have lived with your mother, father, and sisters. I feel uneasy. My heart is not one with them. You told me when I came back to you I would not have to live with them. Yet here we are like beaten dogs with tails between our legs.''

''Perhaps something will happen soon,'' said Mariano. ''Domingo and my father spend more and more of their time negotiating with the government agent. They say a federal order has come which says a Chamula may worship any way he pleases. They are excited about this and seem to have little time to work on what they call translation. *Señor* Jacobs has asked me to help him. I don't understand all he wants me to do but our hearts are warm toward each other. He says I think well before I speak. But what is better is that he will pay me for the work I do.''

And for several weeks it *was* better. Mariano and Estumina found a temporary hut on a small ranch on the outskirts of Las Casas. In the late afternoon of the first day alone they walked together arm in arm. He bought her fruit and they ate in silence—in that cozy world of rekindled love.

''Here I am,'' said Estumina. ''I am yours, take me.'' Mariano felt like a young stallion kicking up his heels in spring after a winter in the barn. The distance that had built up over the months was gone. They loved where they found themselves as if they had never loved before.

As the weeks passed, Mariano began to work longer and longer on translation. Ken found that Mariano possessed a lively, thoughtful mind with fresh insights about how best to translate Scripture concepts into the Chamula Tzotzil language. When Ken realized he had a natural gift for translation, he suggested that Mariano and Estumina move into a two-room brick house on the edge of his property.

But with the move came a new set of problems. It wasn't that Mariano and Estumina were not alone. They were, at least most of the time. The displaced believers were now living in Las Casas in houses of their own or had returned to Chamula. It was true there were often many visitors who came to talk with Ken Jacobs and receive medical attention from Elaine's skilled hands. And occasionally a Chamula family slept on the floor by the fireplace in the room where Estumina cooked Mariano's tortillas and boiled his coffee and soup. But this wasn't the problem. The problem was Mariano. At night he brooded over the Scripture he and Ken had talked about and translated during the day.

One night, after several weeks of constant Scripture translation, Mariano sat on a short, three-legged stool and peered into the dying flame of Estumina's cooking fire. "Who does this God of *Señor* Jacobs think He is?" he said angrily.

"What do you mean?" asked Estumina.

"I mean, if it is as *Señor* Jacobs says that God has made us as we are, then why does He demand that if I have a desire to sin with my hand it would be better to cut it off than go into Hell with two hands?"

"Such strange and frightening words," Estumina said. "Where do they come from?"

"They come from the Book of God from a man named Mark," said Mariano. "We know there is a lower world where the bad spirits live. *Señor* Jacobs says that Jesus Christ died so that we don't have to go into that world he calls Hell."

"Why don't you believe what *Señor* Jacobs and Domingo have told you about letting this Jesus become your Helper?" said Estumina.

"Because I believe the laws of God will be chains to my uncooperative body," said Mariano. In angry frustration he slapped his hand on his knee, stood up, and walked to the small chin-high window.

"I resent this God Who made me with desires, then restricts me from doing what I want," he said. "I reject this! I won't regard this new Book. Who do they think they are? I'll return to San Juan and gain eternal life through my own Chamula system."

"But if you do," said Estumina, "you must live the *whole* system."

Mariano groaned and walked back to their raised plank bed. He knew Estumina was right. He realized he could never fully satisfy all the requirements of the Chamula system. At the same time, he was frightened of going to Hell. The fear was not new. He had always lived wondering if he had offended one of the many animistic Chamula spirits. Now he was being asked to consider and understand that the true God, as *Señor* Jacobs called Him, was unlike any of the long line of gods the Chamulas bowed to in the church of San Juan Chamula.

He was repeatedly frustrated in his struggle to find love and acceptance, yet here was a God Who was reputed to love him, his wife, and all people everywhere above life itself—a God who had been punished for his sin; a God who would be his Helper and Who wanted him to understand that he, Mariano Gomez Hernandez, had been fashioned in God's image and was being offered the opportunity to become an adopted son of the Most High God.

Finally, after several weeks of agonizing inner debate, Mariano concluded that he was a man without hope unless he squarely confronted the challenge of Mark 9:43-49:

> If your hand does wrong, cut it off. Better to live forever with one hand than be thrown into the unquenchable fires of hell with two! If your foot carries you toward evil, cut it off! Better to be lame and live forever than have two feet that carry you to hell. And if your eye is sinful, gouge it out. Better enter the Kingdom of God half blind than have two eyes and see the fires of hell, where the worm never dies, and the fire never goes out—where all are salted with fire.

Alone in a nearby woods, Mariano reflected on all he had learned about this true God and His Son. "Can it be? Is it really true that I am loved, that I have worth, that I am not animal as the *ladino cashlans* say I am? Is there truly Someone to help me stop sinning?"

"Lord," said Mariano out loud, "what do you want me to do?"

And in that moment, Mariano discovered that all the requirements of Scripture were met in Jesus Christ and he took hold of the Helper, as did Estumina some weeks later.

Chapter

9

IT WILL STAY
BY MEANS
OF ME

It Will Stay By Means of Me

All ten men sat in a semicircle under a corrugated iron roof. Most tilted back on their three-legged wooden stools and child-size chairs to look intently at Mariano. Behind them a cavalcade of white moth-butterflies skipped and danced through a patch of cabbage plants. Just outside the circle of men, a young Chamula mother knelt in the grass and nursed her child while her older child—perhaps two and a half or three—cocked her head to one side and twisted her fingers around a tag end of her soiled blouse.

In all, it was a pleasant warm day. A day made for lazy reflection, to become alive to all the sounds of earth. If any of these ten Christian Chamula lay-preachers heard the miniature buzz saw sounds of flies and bees, or the excited chirping of black-throated sparrows, or the twittering of a flamboyant, vermilion flycatcher, they didn't show it. Their eyes and interest were riveted on Mariano's strong, enthusiastic words.

"My brother," said one man, "why is it that your words about the elders and God's Word are different than your father Miguel?"

"I tell you only truths I know the Lord has taught me," said Mariano. "Some of you know it now makes almost ten years since I first learned that God declared me just and perfect in His sight because of His Son, Jesus Christ. In these years I have learned we should love and not hate or fight the elders. We should respect them and pay the tribute when they ask. Some of the earlier believers thought we should always complain to the authorities when they did us wrong. Now I learn from God's Word that we must let God fight our battles. He will keep us according to His best judgment.

"When some of the presidents learned what we believed, they thought it was an insult against the gods and began to persecute us. They believed our new way would bring catastrophe upon all Chamulas. It is for this reason they sought to kill us. And you know that there is still a fear among some brothers that they could still be killed for their faith.

"Yet," continued Mariano, "I am more fearful of displeasing the Lord than all the fury the elders throw at me. We must not be afraid of those who can kill the body. We must fear God. It is He who determines when we shall die, not the elders. Scripture tells us that all things are ours—this means even death is ours. It is therefore impossible for anyone to kill you before God says you can come Home. You yourself cannot make the length of your life an hour longer.

"As you teach in your settlements about the Good

New Words, remind them that God never acts against us. He does not deal with us according to our sin. Also, we must understand we cannot fight or handle our sin alone. God teaches us the help we need to handle sin is in His Son, Jesus Christ. Yet when we do sin, we must learn God still loves us. It was in the darkest hour of my life—in the hour of my adultery—that I learned how much God loved me. I will tell you . . . ."

For almost a year after Mariano accepted God's offer of love and eternal life, friction between the elders and Christians ebbed and flowed like a daily tide. Then suddenly public attention shifted from the Christians to those who had called for their death.

In an unprecedented people's movement, the Chamula nation rose up as one against the elders and president. In a bone-chilling display of force, thousands of Chamula men armed with machetes and guns marched to the *cabildo* in the plaza of San Juan Chamula to protest the heavy tax collection and call for Xalic's death.

Not since the race wars of 1867-69 under the impulsive leadership of Pedro Diaz Cuscat had the Chamula nation rebelled with such furious determination. Then, Cuscat began his revolution with a mandate to the president and elders to defend and preserve the Chamula tribal system against all who threatened to dilute or destroy.

"It is time to finish with the people who are not of our blood, whose soul is not the same as ours, and who have not the same language or customs as ours," Cuscat said in a wild, impassioned speech. "If we don't do this our household gods who live among us will not protect us!''

With the crowd frantically applauding his every word, Cuscat proposed a further notion. ''We don't have to worship an image that represents persons who don't belong to our race. It will soon be time to celebrate the crucifixion. I propose we crucify someone from our town, one who has our same soul and blood.''

And that's precisely what they did. Domingo Gomez Checheb, a young man from the town of San Juan Chamula, was selected and in a ceremony befitting the occasion, died in searing pain on a cross in the settlement of Tzajal-Hemel.

For over 100 years the presidents and elders fanned these passionate ideals into flame whenever they felt their traditions in danger of desecration or when they felt the people might suffer exploitation from the *cashlan*.

But now in a strange reversal, the people shifted their focus from the Christian ''threat'' to what they believed was a greater threat—a president and elder system who demanded too much and had gone too far.

The fury of the crowd was eventually diffused with a promise to reduce taxes and the subsequent arrest of Xalic. The Christians welcomed this shift of interest and began rebuilding their lives.

Mariano's interest in translation grew from indifference to eager affection. On the surface it appeared that peace and tranquility had at last come to Mariano and Estumina. He had a house to live in, good work to do, food to eat, and his wife by his side. But all was not as it appeared.

For reasons unknown to Mariano, Estumina began

bringing up the shame she felt at his outwitting her father and taking his money. At first Mariano apologized. Later when Estumina continued, Mariano fought back and accused her of being at fault.

"It was you who sat there with a closed mouth," said Mariano. "If you had opened your mouth, your father would not have been cut as deeply as he was. But why don't we share the blame? Then we can push it aside and have each other without this hatred."

But Estumina remained inconsolable and coldly unresponsive whenever Mariano felt amorous. Then one day it all exploded.

"It is a lie that you say you love me," said Estumina.

"But it is a truth that I love you," answered Mariano.

"No, it is a lie. I told you over three market days ago that I saw it well that blouse I showed you. Now, because you have not bought me that nice blouse, my body is not yours. And you can't send me out because this house we live in is not your house."

Mariano gritted his teeth. All his conditioning of how a Chamula man should treat an uncooperative wife pulsed through his veins like red liquid in a thermometer when touched by a lighted match. Inside he wanted to hit her but by sheer force of will, he clenched his fist and strode outside.

He walked into the garden with sad, heavy steps. He felt as if he was suffocating in a sea of mud. Again the door of his identity slammed shut, his selfhood extinguished, stomped on, crushed. There was at once pain and hatred and because he had not yet learned how to be sensitive to his wife's needs, felt only the need to be comforted and to give his love away to someone who would understand him, who would smile and laugh with him, and he found her. Juana—seventeen, dimpled, lively, and with eyes perhaps a bit too flirtatious. She had come to live in Ken's yard while her parents relocated in Las Casas. At that moment it was born in Mariano's heart to take her.

As the weeks passed, Mariano's responsibility toward the translation of the Chamula New Testament increased. So also did his budding talent to teach some of the new truths he was learning from Scripture. Yet there existed a rocking in his heart.

He wanted and needed Estumina, and in reality, she him. But his manhood was at stake, and her pride was at stake—and the rocking in his heart increased. The growing feelings of estrangement toward Estumina and the excitement and liberation he found in Juana seemed to violate what he was beginning to learn from Scripture, but the rocking increased.

One night, Juana asked Estumina and Mariano if she could sleep in their house by the fireplace as it was warmer than the clinic where she slept. After they all had talked and retired, Mariano began to allow the frustrations of the past weeks to run through his mind. "I hurt . . . my manhood is being violated . . . Estumina holds herself from me . . . Juana likes me . . . she understands me . . . my manhood . . . I hear her breathing . . . she laughs with me . . . Estumina quarrels . . . Juana laughs . . . my manhood . . . ."

And in the night Mariano went to her, and she did not resist.

For a long time, Mariano stood by the window of the tiny, brick study in the garden where he and Ken worked. He watched the rain fall and run off the tile roof of the chicken coop and trickle into little puddles in the garden. With his eyes fixed on the cluster of old fruit trees out-side, Mariano spoke. "Brother Ken, ever since I read the words in Mark I have desired to live right before God. But the more I try to stop myself, the more I find myself attracted to the very thing I don't want to do."

Over the months of working together, the friendship between this tall, sensitive translator from Minnesota and the equally sensitive Mariano grew without words. Both men loved and deeply respected each other and worked as colleagues in a common God-given task.

Ken had known about Mariano's moral lapse for more than a month. Estumina, who had heard her husband and Juana talking in the night, got up and in a stomach-wrenching scene, found them together. In the morning she tearfully told all to Elaine. This had not been the first time such a problem had occurred among some of the Chamula men who were emerging as Christian leaders. But always before when it happened, they fled and left the group of believers who were now meeting for regular church and study services. Ken's hope was that Mariano's hurt would be so deep he would bring it up first and not run away. He wanted to be available to help him. "Perhaps this will be the day," thought Ken.

He was about to tell Mariano that all men including the Apostle Paul struggled with this same dilemma when Mariano said, "Brother Ken, I do not think I will be able to continue working on the letters of John." Ken felt a hot flush in his cheeks and decided to press the issue.

"Why, my brother, would you want to leave me?" said Ken gently.

Mariano turned and looked down at Ken who sat in a straight, wooden chair at their mutual desk. "I will leave because I think you may no longer want me."

Ken stood up and laid his hand on Mariano's shoulder. "No, no, brother. I have never said I don't want you. But why is it that I see you sad?"

In that instant, Mariano's tears came like a hot, wet rain driven by a wind from the fountains of his soul. They pelted across his mind and splattered and cracked like glass marbles on the pavement of his body. "Oh, brother," he sobbed, "I have sinned."

"What have you done?" asked Ken.

"I slept with Juana," said Mariano, then hastened to add, "but only once. Now because I have not done what God's Word demands, I believe I must be punished and go to Hell. I am afraid."

Ken wanted to jump in and reassure Mariano that God still loved and cared for him, that there had never been a time when God had never loved him, but decided to let Mariano continue talking.

"There are those who know of my sin. They look at me and point and say, 'There goes a sinner.' And here I am in the process of telling others about the Good New Words and I have deep shame.

"I have a problem with my wife and I struggle with bad thoughts. Nothing I do has any flavor. Everything I do and everything I touch is bitter. It is as if someone was saying to me, 'There is no hope for you. You are doomed to Hell. You will never see the goodness of life, your body is too wicked. Hell is your destiny.' This, my brother, is how I feel. Like I am in a cave with no way out."

"If you believe in your heart and mind that Jesus is

the Christ, God's Son and your Helper (Saviour)," said Ken, "then you are God's child forever. He will never send you to Hell. But you must go to God in prayer and tell Him what you have told me. Only then when you admit your sin before Him can He give you back the joy you had when you first knew Him."

For a week after his confession to Ken, Mariano struggled unsuccessfully to reconcile the weakness of his body to the desires of his mind. Then late one afternoon, alone in the study, Mariano began talking to God and reading the Chamula version of Romans he and Ken had been translating.

Mariano held the typewritten manuscript to the light of the window and read verses 21 and 22 of Romans, chapter two.

> But take a good look at what you really are like. You teach others but that's all you do. You fail to teach yourself. You tell others not to steal, but you steal yourself.
>
> You tell others not to commit adultery, but you commit adultery. You tell others . . . .

Mariano stopped and reread the first part of verse 22. It was as if someone spoke directly to him and said, "THAT IS YOU!" But Mariano said to himself, "No, that couldn't be me," and lay the manuscript on the desk. He thought for awhile, then picked it up and read chapter three.

Words like verse 12 and others penetrated deeply into his heart, mind and soul.

> Every person walks away from the presence of God. All activities of every person are of no use to

God. Not a single person does that which is good. All do evil.

Not a single person understands what steps are necessary so that we may have inner peace together.

Therefore, not a single person is seen well by God for having obeyed the law. Look, the law only serves to demonstrate to us that we are sinners.

So you who are in Christ, you are joined together along with other believers to make a large house in which God lives by means of the Holy Spirit who is in you.

But now God has made it known to us the conditions under which we are seen well by God. They are not by means of the law. To be seen well by God is only through faith in Jesus Christ. These conditions to be seen well by God are what Moses and the prophets wrote about because we are all sinners, no one has a righteous heart that reaches the same level as God.

Even though we are like that, God decided to save us. Therefore, without price or payment on our part, we are seen well by God because He Himself has saved us through Jesus Christ.

Therefore God sent Jesus Christ to die so in this way we gain pardon from sin by means of faith in Jesus Christ.

These verses warmed his heart but he could not get away from verse 22 of chapter two and he went back to it and began talking to God.

"God, here I am and I don't know what Your Words demand. I am in trouble and I don't know where I am at. Is it true that I am like this Word says I am?''

Mariano stood up and walked to the window and looked outside. Something inside seemed to say, ''MARIANO, YOU ARE RIGHT. YOU ARE LIKE THIS WORD SAYS.''

''Is it true? Is it true, O God? Is that what I am, O God? You are right. I am what You say I am. But what can be done? I cannot of myself give up this sin.''

Again, God seemed to say to Mariano, ''DON'T BE AFRAID. I WILL HELP YOU.''

''But what can I do? You know that this is the way of my heart.''

''HERE I AM. THE MOMENT YOU COME TO ME, I WILL HELP YOU.''

''But, Lord, will it stay by means of me (can I keep my faith and learn to obey God's commands?)?''

''BY MEANS OF ME IT WILL STAY. BY MEANS OF ME YOU CAN DO IT. BY YOURSELF, YOU CAN'T.''

A few white moth-butterflies still flitted in and out of the cabbage patch as Mariano paused for a moment to catch his breath.

''Brother,'' said one of the young men, ''don't stop now. What happened? What did you say to God? And what of Estumina?''

Mariano smiled. ''I was exhausted and it was late. Later than I knew when I finished reading and praying. It seemed God was saying to me I was to depend on His strength, not on my strengh, and I said, 'Let it be thus.' In this way, brothers, did I begin to come out of my sin. In this way I was convinced that God was saying to me, 'Here I am. I have come to free you of everything you can't undo yourself. I am your Helper and I will give you freedom.'

"Later I read a verse in the letters of John. It said if I am afraid of God I will wrongly think in my heart that He wants to punish me. But He loves me, and because of my faith in Jesus, His Son, He has nothing against me. I have been forgiven and it is for this reason I can tell you about my sin. God declares that I am seen well by Him, and He declares you seen well by Him because of your faith in His Son."

"And what of Estumina?" asked the brethren.

"Ah," said Mariano, "that is a story for the next time we meet. Then I will tell you how I had to unlearn all I was taught about how a Chamula man should treat his wife."

Chapter
10

IT IS WITH ONE HEART I SLEEP

It Is with One Heart I Sleep

As Mariano allowed the truth of Scripture to work in his life, he began to celebrate and share what had been won for him. He was a new person in Jesus Christ. As such it gave him a radical new freshness and authority to affirm others as important in their own right. His non-threatening witness was a powerful instrument of love and peace and the Chamula believers listened carefully to what he taught from the Scriptures and his own life.

"Brothers," said Mariano, "I have a body just like yours. Sin draws me. I want to sin. But I look at it, and I look at Christ's offer, and I know sin has no reward. So I am learning to say *no* to sin and say *yes* to Christ."

A week had passed since Mariano and the ten Chamula lay-preachers had met for their regular Friday morning study sessions. This week the number had swelled to twenty-two. Many of the men had walked for as long as ten hours on hard, lung-splitting trails to sit and listen to Mariano's ministry from the Word. He had promised to tell them what he had learned from Scripture about how a Chamula man should treat his wife and how he and Estumina were reconciled. But first he reminded them that while sin from a distance looks pleasant and for the moment seems to satisfy the pain of being human, its ultimate end is always pain, disappointment and shame.

"For many weeks after my sin I wondered how I could practice (live) right so God would accept me. As I read the Scriptures I stopped where in Romans it talks about adultery. The Word of God in our Chamula language was like a finger pointing right at me. I took the Scriptures, read it, then put it down and said to myself, 'Is this my nature? Am I one who looks for women?' Then I again picked up the Scriptures and the same words came to me, 'YOU ARE AN ADULTERER.' 'No I am not,' I would say. Then again I would lay the Scriptures down and think, 'Is this the way my heart really is?'

"Yet only when I admitted what I was before God did I hear Him say, 'THE MOMENT YOU COME TO ME I AM HERE TO HELP YOU.' But after this I wondered how I could ever practice right so God would accept me. As I read the Scripture Brother Ken and I translated, it came to me, 'MARIANO, I LOVE YOU. THROUGH CHRIST YOU ARE SEEN WELL BY ME.'

"But I would argue with God and say, 'After what I've done You can't see me well.' And again the inner voice would say, 'YES I DO SEE YOU WELL. I SEE YOU HAVE A STRAIGHT HEART.'

"As I continued to study, it came to me I could never please God by practicing—by the efforts of my body. I was seen well and was free because the Good New Words are not an *order*. It is an *offer* that I must respond to. I am free because God says I am. Now when I meet people who hate me I can tell them I love them. I am free not to hate!

"Sometimes I would pray, 'Lord, help. Lord, keep me. Lord, don't throw me out of Your heart.' Don't pray like that. God has promised to do all these things. Pray rather for God to make you honest before Him and yourself. If you do, and step into God's light, He will show you what your true heart is. When He does, agree with God that He is right. This is what I did with Estumina.

"After I saw from Scripture I was free, that God loved me, I assumed my wife was also listening and understanding the Word of God. Not once did I talk to her about my intimate experience with God, nor did I help her in the house. When things went wrong and she cried for help, all I said was, 'This is what the Lord is for. He is here to help you.' But never once did I tell her what I had found in my heart.

"Many months went by and I wasn't helping her. Then at a retreat study session like this, I heard that Christian husbands should learn to help their wives understand the Scriptures and help them with things they don't understand. I said in my heart, 'Ah, not me. This is what she has the Lord for. Why should I help her?'

"One day I began to see my relationship with my wife and family was wrong. It came to me that she was of no use to me. Nothing was going good in my house and maybe we ought to separate.''

Mariano paused for a moment to make sure they were paying attention. They were!

"You see, brothers," he continued, "I was free of one sin but still not free from another kind of sin. I was thinking only of myself. One day I walked out through the fruit trees in Brother Ken's yard and asked the Lord what was necessary that I do. 'Lord,' I said, 'here I am in Your presence. Let me know what is in Your heart as it relates to Estumina and me. There is not a good thing that I gain from having someone like her. I am not one hearted with my wife. Here is my hand. Lead me so I will know what I will have to do with her.'

"And God seemed to speak and say, 'TEACH HER AND LET HER KNOW HOW I HELPED YOU. ONLY WITH YOUR MIND DO YOU LOVE YOUR WIFE. YOU DO NOT SEE HER WELL FROM THE INSIDE OF YOUR HEART.'

"There in His presence I agreed with God and said, 'You are right. I don't see her well,' and I told the Lord exactly what I felt in my heart toward Estumina. I said, 'Estumina is not a nice young girl anymore. She is getting older. She doesn't serve me (give me her body) like she did before.'

"Brothers, I was honest before God and told Him everything that was in my heart. Then I said, 'Lord, is there room for change in my life?' And the Lord said, 'GIVE TO ME WHAT IS IN YOUR HEART.' And I said, 'Let it be thus.'

"I went to Estumina and said, 'Estumina, there have been many days that I haven't seen you well. Will you give me pardon?' And Estumina said, 'Yes, it is true. I have seen it. There have been many days since you have loved me.' And I said, 'Estumina, with the help of the Lord I will love you again.' And Estumina came to me and put her arms around my neck and said, 'Man, your sin is gone.'

"You know how most of our marriages are miserable. We react in hatred against our wives when they burn tortillas or say they are too tired to lay with us. There is nothing we see that is good and we treat them badly just to get the hate out of our hearts. This is because we have been taught that a woman is good only to provide for our needs. Now as I read the Scriptures I find I must unlearn all I was taught about how I should treat my wife. The Scriptures teach me that my purpose for taking a woman as I look at her and say I want her, is not to make my life happy or well-off. I choose her and give myself for her to make *her* well-off by me, like Christ in love gave Himself for *my* welfare. As she senses and knows this, she submits and responds to my love. Now up to this very day my family is happy, we are free, and my heart explodes with happiness."

With deep conviction and enthusiasm, Mariano continued to teach and press home the fresh new concepts he had learned from Scripture.

"The other key to loving my wife was that I asked her pardon for my sin. When I had sinned and knew before God I was no good, He helped me. Now I can see my wife with her inabilities and faults and love her as Christ loves her. And I see I must help her as Christ helps me. Remember, brothers, the key to a good marriage relationship is to love your wife and help her."

Mariano's ability as an energetic storyteller, an able minister and witness for his Lord became well known among the growing Chamula church. Yet his witness was never abrasive and seldom did he initiate a conversation about the Lord. But when the opportunity arose, he readily explained why his life-style had changed. Like the time he sat under a tall oak tree in a market and wisely made the village barber eager to learn his "secret of happy life."

"Man, you are fat (healthy, robust, clear-eyed)," said the barber.

"Do you want to be fat like me?" asked Mariano.

"Oh, I'd love to be fat like you," said the barber. "Tell me, what medicines do I have to buy to be fat like you?"

The corners of Mariano's mouth turned up into a mischievous smile as he shook his head. "It is not a medicine."

"Ah, don't deceive me," said the barber.

"Okay," said Mariano, "there is a medicine. There are beans and onions and potatoes, and you can eat a little meat. These will make you fat."

"Stop deceiving me," said the barber.

"No, what I say is the truth," said Mariano.

"No, no, stop deceiving me. Tell me the truth of how I see you fat and happy and without conflicts."

"Do you really want to hear?" asked Mariano.

"I want to hear!" said the barber with eyes wide open.

"Okay, I will tell you," said Mariano. "You see me fat and you see me happy, but it is not food that does this to me. It is the Lord God. He is my Helper."

With a warm smile and shining eyes, Mariano leaned closer to the barber. His words were clear, calm, deliberate and without hesitation. Gently he pointed his index finger at the barber's chest.

"The One who helped me is the Lord; the One who died on the cross for both of us. He is the One who helps me. He set me free from liquor. He set me free from my deep desire for women. And he set me free from the fear of being cursed by the *bruja*. Now when I go to bed it is with one heart I sleep. I am at peace. It is for this reason I am fat.

"And this is the very same thing you can get for yourself. Therefore, my friend barber, if you come to realize what is in the heart of God concerning you, you can say you are a son of God even though you don't see Him before you. But you must understand when our Lord died on the cross it was to blot out your sins like a cloud when it vanishes.

"Our Lord did this because He loves you and wants to bring you out of the hand of death and Hell. And in the end, He desires to take you to a new land where you can live forever with Him in happiness.

"But our Lord also died for the purpose that you should live well now. Look at me. Before I heard about the Lord, I did everything my own heart wanted, just like you are doing. And I was like you, Barber, bound by sin.

"There is no reason in the world that you can't be free from your sin when you take seriously what Christ did for you. If you do, your relationship with your family, your conduct, and your relationship with other people will change with His help."

The barber was silent for a long time, then muttered something about not being sure if he would be happy in this new way. Mariano knew what it was like to be puzzled with such strange new words. He knew how hard it was for a Chamula to change a lifetime of deeply ingrained thinking and social patterns. But he also knew a secret, and he wanted to share it.

"Barber," said Mariano, "don't you want to be well off? Don't you want peace? Don't you want freedom from fear? Don't you want a happy heart?"

"I want this," said the barber simply.

"Then take it," said Mariano. "God is giving it to you. You have seen of me and you said you want it. I obtained it from the Lord. This is what Christ has given me. You, barber, can be well-off by Him, too. Let us go into the presence of the Lord. I will take you there."

And the barber went and that same day was "seen well by the Lord."

With all his enthusiasm, logic and force, sometimes Mariano's words were still treated with indifference and he needed special help. After the elders signed a tentative peace treaty, a number of believers returned to their settlements to live and farm their land. But they were never totally free from harassment. One night a gang of ten men decided to frighten a Christian family by rolling a large clay water jug down a hill in front of their house.

The plan was for the men to shoot the Christians as they came outside to investigate the noise made by the breaking jug. But as the jug began to roll, a strange phenomenon occurred. Instead of the noise frightening the believers, for some unexplainable reason it frightened the ten men.

A would-be killer's wife later told Mariano and some of the believers what her husband reported: "As the jug rolled toward the house it seemed as if the noise grew louder and louder, like growing thunder. Then from out of the darkness we saw people standing with guns pointed right at us. We were all so intensely scared, we ran, without looking, into the trees and bushes, scratching our legs and tearing our *chamarras*.''

"When my husband told me this," said the woman, "I said, 'You can't kill them. They have their own Lord who watches them—their own spiritual protector who is a fearsome thing.' ''

After the woman finished her story, Mariano carefully explained how she might also have this same Lord to protect and watch over her.

"It is too difficult to trust in what you are saying," said the woman, and turned and left. But that night she had a dream in which she heard someone say, "Is it not truth he is telling you? Is he not worthy to believe? Does he not tell you where there is help? Regard seriously what is being told to you."

And in the days ahead the woman came to seriously regard what Mariano had told her and God became her Helper and Spiritual Protector.

In 1964, there were only two Chamula men— Domingo and Miguel—who said they would follow the Good New Words. A year later there were 35. Between the years 1965 to 1969, the number of Chamulas who wanted this new hope grew to over 120, the persecution notwithstanding.

In the early 70's there was a period of uneasy calm punctuated by periodic harassment. The elders knew there were too many believers to exterminate as they had once hoped. But they still could not bring themselves to a peaceful coexistence. In 1974 another wave of persecution jailed almost two hundred Chamula Christians and drove still dozens more from their homes. But a year before this extreme measure, Mariano was summoned to appear before the elders at the *cabildo*.

Chapter
11

YOU MAKE
THAT CHOICE

You Make that Choice

The president sat behind his pine table clutching his silver topped staff. A dozen elders and other officials flanked his sides while Mariano stood silent before them. A growing crowd stood in the doorways outside.

It was reminiscent of several years before when he stood before the president and elders to be questioned about his treatment of Estumina. Then, the president and elders were favorably disposed to help him recover his wife. Now, Mariano sensed from the council a mixture of bewilderment, anger, fear, and in some, a tinge of admiration, like one has for a brave adversary.

In an eloquent speech designed more for the crowd and elders than Mariano and those believers who accompanied him, the president warmed to his subject as he saw his audience nod their heads in agreement.

"Here you see us, brothers of San Juan. We are the

elders, the little fathers of our patron saint. Remember, it is our patron saint who sends the rain. He gives us the sun and gentle breezes—everything that pertains to life. It is San Juan who when he sees we have not pushed aside the traditions of our ancestors, responds to the welfare of our beans, our corn, our cabbages, potatoes, and peas. Without him we would not have these things.

"Sons of San Juan, there has come among us another authority that does not follow the rules we say must be followed. This new authority says everyone must decide for himself how he should live. But to do this is to violate tribal authority."

The president stopped and in a taunting nod of his head said, "Therefore, Mariano, tell us where did you learn this new authority? Where did you learn all the things you tell those who follow this new way? Tell us how it is that you no longer regard highly those things that have come to us from the past. I am told, Mariano, that you are a wise man, that you deal with us differently than Domingo and your father, that you no longer go to the government *cashlan* in Las Casas to fight us, and you tell your followers to pay us the tribute. But tell us, how can you be truly wise or settle disputes or give people justice without drinking our holy *posh*? Tell us, we need to know. If you open your heart and tell the truth—fine. If you don't, we will put you and these who have come back to live with us in jail. Now tell us, Mariano. Tell us truly."

"Esteemed President and Elders of our land," said Mariano as he stepped forward to speak, "we are not regarding seriously anything else. The only thing we are believing is about our Lord. There is nothing bad that we do. We do not kill anyone. We do not steal from anyone. The only thing we do is to believe and obey the Good New Words.''

"Yes, what you say is true," said the president, "but you still do not regard San Juan. And if you don't regard him highly, we will all lose our food and you will be driven from our land."

"Before you drive us from our land," said Mariano, "let me speak again. You who are the little fathers of San Juan and call yourselves the sons of god are right. I too and those who follow the Good New Words are also sons of God. And He of whom we say we are His sons is the One we make known to all the Chamulas—the One Who died for us, the One Who paid for us—Jesus Christ.

"Just consider, esteemed President and Elders, our Lord paid for your sins so that you would not have to be lost. And because of our Lord, here I am before you, and wherever I walk through our land I tell them about you, about how your sins are paid."

"But we don't want such a thing!" said the elders and president together.

"But, esteemed Council, why don't you want such a thing when you are the ones that say we should regard highly the Lord of Heaven? We who follow the Good New Words regard highly the Lord of Heaven, the Lord of our tribe, exactly like you. At the fiesta you bow low before the one who is taken out and nailed on a cross (Chamulas have a special fiesta where symbolically a saint is taken from the church and nailed again on the cross). This One Who was nailed on a cross many, many, many years ago is my Lord. And He can be yours, too!

"Esteemed Council, God gave His Son to die on the

cross so that we all would be set free and seen well by Him; so that we should not continue to carry our sin. This sin ultimately brings death but the Good New Words tell us about the work of God. It embraces you—everyone—so that you will never go to eternal death.

"When I was in the presence of sin, I did not think whether the day was nice or not. It was just a day. I looked at the mountains, the caves, the river, but not once did I draw into myself whether it was beautiful or not. It was a river, it was a mountain, this is all I saw in it.

"Now that I am a believer, I experience the freedom that comes through our Lord Jesus Christ and I see wonder, I see beauty, I feel it. Every day that passes has meaning. I go for a walk and I enjoy God's beauty. I even hear things I never heard before!

"Esteemed Council, in the old life the things that should have been beautiful all held fear for me. When I went through the forest I never stopped because I was filled with much fear. Now because the Lord of Heaven has sent Himself personally here to us and has given us the gift of life, I have come out of the presence of being lost and am free!"

Mariano bowed his head and stepped back.

Angrily the president, as if deaf to all he had heard, demanded that Mariano regard seriously their patron saint San Juan and Chamula customs. Of all life's moments, only a few count more than all others—the moment of decision, of choice. Mariano had had an encounter with ideas, but more with a Person. He simply had to shoulder the responsibility of his commitment, and he stepped forward.

"Esteemed President and Council, I and those who follow the new way regard only the Lord who paid for our sins."

The president gritted his teeth and cracked his staff on the pine floor. "Let the dissidents be placed in jail for this day and night!"

Mariano smiled and bowed. "We will not fight you but pray for you and love you as our Lord loves you."

Mariano was what he was—human. People knew he had sinned and they understood him to be a man who knew the sharp contrast between light and darkness. They also knew him as a man who believed and tried to practice what he told others. The Chamula church learned this of Mariano when they heard of his young son's near death by hernia strangulation. It only confirmed in their minds his determined resolve to obey and practice the new truths of Scripture.

Estumina's delivery of their first child, a son, was prefaced by a Chamula midwife rubbing Estumina's abdomen with rattlesnake grease to keep her abdomen soft. Then in a manner of most Chamula births, Mariano stood behind his wife and tightly pulled her sash. In front of Estumina a relative sat on a low chair and gripped Estumina's shoulders to support her during each labor pain.

After the birth, the midwife tied the umbilical cord a hand span from the infant and cut it with the point of a heated machete. When the afterbirth was buried in the yard, the midwife cleaned the child with a dry rag and gave him to his mother.

As Mariano's love for Estumina grew after his deep encounter with the Lord, so grew his love for his son, and later for another son and daughter. He had not forgotten the fear, uncertainty, and pain of his own childhood, of wanting to be loved, of asking for bread and being given a stone. Here now was a chance to give away his love in a sensitive new way and with joy he did.

Yet in the midst of his spiritual struggles and growing responsibilities toward the fledgling Chamula church, Mariano failed to understand the seriousness of his four-year-old son's hernia problem. One day a doctor warned Mariano his son might die or never be able to work if the hernia was not repaired.

As Mariano considered how he would pay for such an operation, he also considered a passage of Scripture in Matthew 17:20 which he and Ken had been translating. There it talked about a person who could move a mountain even if his faith was as small as a grain of mustard.

After the boy had a particularly difficult night, Ken offered to pay for the operation. When Mariano returned later in the afternoon at the time Ken had scheduled to leave, he said, "I have decided not to go."

"But, Brother," said Ken, "you see your son's hernia, how large it is. This is serious. He is almost strangled with it."

"I know that is true," said Mariano, "but I have thought about the Scriptures in Matthew as it relates to my son. There it says if you have faith and take seriously the fact that God wants this mountain to be removed and God intends that it be removed, even though your faith is as little as a grain of mustard seed you can say to Him, 'Let it happen.' And I have prayed."

"What have you prayed?" asked Ken.

"At first I prayed for the Lord to remove the hernia. Then I felt ashamed before God. Not that He made me feel ashamed, but I began to feel it was not my responsibility to tell God what He must do. It was my responsibility to agree with what God has chosen for me. Therefore, I said to God, 'Lord, it is not my work to tell You what to do. If you want to, You can take my son. You make that choice,' and I was free.''

Astonished by the implications of Mariano's decision, Ken nevertheless acquiesced in favor of not disturbing Mariano's simple and sincere piety. For several weeks after Mariano's prayer, his son's hernia condition seemed unchanged. He still had difficulty walking but as the days passed he complained less and less until one day, three months later, an examination revealed no trace of the large hernia that once threatened the child's life.

As Mariano and Ken struck deeper and deeper into the translation of the New Testament, Mariano strove to interpret and appropriate the new concepts for his daily life and Chamula culture. He particularly applied the new things he learned to the resurgence of unrest among the elders and president against the growing number of Chamulas who refused the accepted life-style patterns the council had selected.

"If they kill us, we will not fight back," preached Mariano. "God will keep us according to His best judgment. Therefore let God fight our battles. We will not complain to the outside authorities."

There are two jails in San Juan Chamula. One for men and one for women. The cement and adobe block buildings measure 20 by 20 feet. There is no window, no bed, no chair, no toilet, not even a bucket—nothing.

A prisoner can smoke if someone feels kindly toward him and passes a cigarette through the bars. And if a friend comes to visit, he gives him food because no food is provided. The friend can stand outside the iron door and talk and joke to ease the prisoner's humiliation and pain of isolation.

But on the day a year after Mariano had appeared before the president, the *mayols* brought in 160 believers—all men (their wives and children fled to the hills or Las Casas)—no one felt kindly toward them. The *mayols* let any neighbor who wanted, kick, beat, shove, and verbally abuse the believers as they were crammed sardine-tight into the two small jails.

Almost before it happened, the grapevine told the Las Casas authorities what was happening in San Juan Chamula. To avert what they thought would be a bloodbath, two truckloads of soldiers were sent in to act as mediators. But it took twelve hours without water, without being able to relieve themselves. Twelve hours of hot body contact where each person felt the hot breath of his brother on his neck, on his cheek, and in his mouth.

"A hymn would take away our thinking about the dryness in our throats," said one man.

"Ah, good," said another who was jammed in the middle. "I have a hymnbook in my back pocket but we are so tight I cannot reach it with my hands. Perhaps another could."

And another did, and they sang. They sang of Jesus, of His love and care, His understanding their pain, and of Heaven. And when they had sung all the hymns, the man whose book it was belched with satisfaction, as if he'd had a cold drink of water.

For more than a month after the elders had ordered the dissidents beaten, jailed, and trucked out of Chamula territory, Mariano maintained an almost round-the-clock vigil. He sat on a stool under a tin roof outside his house and prayed, encouraged from the Scriptures, often from original unpublished manuscripts, and counseled a constant stream of Chamula believers. Almost all talked of the recent persecution and jailing. "Brother Ken's yard is full again and still our brothers come. My house, like the house of three others, was burned to the ground. And here I am as you see me with only what my wife and children could carry. Brother Mariano, I am afraid. What words do you have from the Scripture for me?"

"Brother Mariano, it makes almost four weeks since the elders ordered the *mayols* to bring in all the men who follow our Lord. And although I have been jailed and trucked out and we all have been told never to return, I believe God wants me and my family to return. I will trust God and risk the choice of what they that hate us will do. There are still the caves to sleep in at night. Will you pray for us before we return?"

"It is easy for you to sit here all day, and yes, into the night to counsel us. But you weren't there when it happened, when all 160 of us were stuck together with no room to sit, with no place to relieve ourselves, with no water to drink. For twelve hours we stood in that jail. I will never go back."

"I am sorry our brother feels the hatred against the elders. It is as you say, Brother Mariano, better to let God fight our battles. I was there, too. I saw the bleeding feet of the brothers who were stomped on by the *mayols* with their hard leather sandals. Even before we got to jail the *mayols* allowed our neighbors to beat us with their machetes, digging sticks, and hoes. The neighbors said they did this because they despised us for eating dead people and because they believe in our meetings we take each other's wives freely. But I am free not to hate and I will return.''

"It was as you said it was. It was also hot like a great hand over our mouths and nose. But do you remember when we started to sing?"

"Yes, Brother, I remember I too like the others felt refreshed from the singing. But do you remember the brother who could not sing? The beating broke his jaw and his spittle drained from his mouth but he told me the pain left him as we sang!''

Some time later when Ken and Elaine offered coffee and a simple cookie to this little man and his wife, each bowed their heads and gave thanks. For three minutes they prayed, thanking God that they were His children. They ended their prayer with, ''Lord, give back to these our brother and sister, the replacement for whatever they have used to feed us. This is all we will tell you now.''

Like her husband, Estumina also encouraged the women who crowded into her 12 by 12 foot kitchen, dining, guest, bed and family room to cook their tortillas and boil their coffee over her small wall fireplace. But like Mariano, Estumina found few who were discouraged. This disturbance was unlike the persecution several years earlier when she and Mariano had fled with his family. Then, most were disillusioned and bitter. Now, no one talked of revenge. Rather, they found a new kind of love. The kind that comes through shared struggle.

In the beginning, only two men followed the Good New Words. But now each Sunday 150 to 200 believers met in the hall of the Presbyterian church in Las Casas. It wasn't that the pain of separation from their home wasn't as real as before. It was. Each one struggled with the pain of separation from their extended families, and they suffered from the exasperation of being misunderstood. But now for the first time they examined their individual lives and priorities and began to understand there was meaning and value in suffering. Some saw that there is no life without it.

Chapter

12

IN THE
PROCESS OF
SUCCEEDING

In the Process of Succeeding

There were two hundred who met in Ken Jacob's yard on the Sunday before they all left for their homes in Chamula. The white moth-butterflies were there, too. A gentle breeze blew cotton ball clouds across a rich blue sky. Sometimes the clouds blotted out the warmth of the sun and the nursing mothers drew their shawls around their babies.

"I have asked you all to come together for this last time to hear what words I would say to you," said Mariano. He then read and commented at length from the twelfth chapter of Luke. He warned them of the dangers of hypocrisy, of not taking God seriously, then said, "You know what I am and what I am like. There is no point in telling you over again. You know sin has no reward. But we can't in our own strength obey the teachings of Jesus. We need Him as our Helper.

Remember to tell those who consider the Good New Words that there isn't a single law of God which they or any of us can keep without His help. If we are to love, we can't. If we are not to steal, we can't. If we are not to lust, we can't. We can't keep from these things. We need to go to God and say, 'Will you be responsible to run my life?' When he offers His help, take it. You will be free and seen well by God because of His Son.

"As you return it will be for some at the risk of death. I too will return as soon as all the Good New Words of the New Testament are put into our Chamula language. If any of you are killed, it is the responsibility of those who remain to bury the dead. You are not to retaliate. God is the One who has set the elders in authority over us, therefore we must pray for them. They are part of God's plan. No man can snuff out our lives before it is time. God is in control and He always works for our good. It is impossible for anyone to kill us before God says we can come home. If we are killed by them, let us consider since God is over all, this is part of His will.

"Remember then, God has made Himself responsible to take us to His goal for our lives and will give us what He has planned for us. This is our hope. This is what we live for. Now let us pray for the brother whose wife has died and who needs our encouragement.

"Our Lord, You have committed to heaven what has pleased you. It is not our work to tell You what to do. The power is in Your hands. We are in Your control. We are Yours, Your children. Therefore, Lord, here is Your son, the one who stays, the one who has lost his companion. O Lord, open our understanding. Help us to know what we can do for our suffering brother. Give us Your wisdom to know what we can do so that we can know how to make life easier for our brother in his loss.

"His heart hurts, the pain continues, he is sad. Our Lord, we desire of You that You give us words to encourage our brother so that in this way, by means of Your intervention, the hurt of his heart and the pain he feels will be administered to by You. There is no one who can really give peace and comfort to our hearts. You are the only One. Let it be thus."

Two years later in 1976, in spite of aggressive threats from the president and elders and nine years after Domingo and Miguel first responded to God's offer of eternal life, over one thousand Chamula believers meet for Bible study, prayer and hymn singing in 30 settlements. Ken and Elaine Jacobs have completed the translation of the Chamula New Testament and as of this writing, Mariano is building a house in San Juan Chamula on a piece of land given to him by his father—this in face of warnings that he could be killed if he returned. His only response is, "I feel the time has come for me to go back."

While he builds, he continues to share himself and the truth the Holy Spirit reveals to him out of his study of Scripture. As the Chamula church grows, so grows his reputation as a wise, sensitive, spiritual leader, a leader who intuitively interprets the Christian gospel. Not in a North American fashion, but as a true Chamula.

When a woman heard of his son's healing, she brought her own sick child to him for prayer. "Brother Mariano," she implored, "pray for my sick child."

Unsmiling, Mariano stroked his chin, turned on his heel, and walked away from her in thoughtful silence. After walking in a large circle, he returned to the woman and said, "Sister, you want me to be your witch doctor. You want me to get God to do for me what you think He won't do for you. It is not my job to pray and beg God to heal your child. Why don't you go to Him? He will do for you what He will do for me, and He will not do any more for me than He will do for you. It is not our work to tell God what to do. It is our responsibility to agree with what God has chosen for us."

His approach for sharing the Good New Words with others is, "Don't tell a person what he needs to do. First tell him about God. A man must first hear about God's offer, about who God is, and what God says He will do for him.

"I ask a person to imagine the Lord standing before him saying, 'Man, understand, I have made myself responsible to handle your sin. If you try to handle your sin or do something about it, you are not listening to what I have said. Before you heard about me you tried to handle your own sin by performing religious duties, but I have come to handle it for you. By my life, by my death, and by my resurrection are your sins handled. I make myself responsible to help govern your life from the inside out. I do this by writing the words of my laws on your heart and mind. I have not come to impose a law on you or make you walk alone. Rather I make myself responsible to help you!'

"And the last thing I say is this—if you want this offer, say to the Lord, 'Thank you. This is what I want.' "

When twenty men chosen for church leadership

discussed the mode and method of baptism they should adopt, Mariano listened. For almost an hour the men debated the issue. Said one, "Since baptism is just a sign of an inward work, let us sprinkle. In this way none will be offended. If our women are put into the water by another man, they will be embarrassed. They will also be embarrassed because they will have to wear different clothes." And some said, "Yes, let's do it this way."

Finally Mariano stood up. "Brethren," he said, "I have listened to all of you talk and I haven't heard one of you say, 'In my heart this is what God is telling me to do.' Maybe this is just Mariano talking, but I want to tell you what is in my heart. I have been alone with God trying to listen to what He is saying. I feel He wants me to go down into the water and to come up out of the water. Now I may change, but I want you to know this is what the Holy Spirit has taught me."

During the 1976 Easter Sunday celebrations after a day of preaching, singing and feasting in the woods, 800 Chamula believers met in the yard of the Las Casas Presbyterian church to see the film *King of Kings*. When it was over, Mariano stood by a microphone and said, "Consider this picture we have seen and how it shows us we have come out from the presence of being lost. God felt hurt in His heart over us and did a work for us so that we will never see or appear before the place of pain (hell).

"He is merciful to us. His mercy has nothing to do with anything we have given Him. It is His gift to us. Therefore encourage all those who do not yet understand how they can be free."

He then suggested that if there were those who felt the Lord speaking to them, they come out of the crowd to the microphone and lead in prayer. And they came—by the dozens. Paxcu came—the only woman to do so—while her young husband cuddled their new baby. Many prayers revealed a growing insight of how deeply and passionately Jesus loved them. For two hours they came and prayed until finally Mariano suggested that since the hour was late they should break up and go home. But no one wanted to go home. As the Spirit of God moved among them, they embraced and wept together, rejoicing in God's love for them.

Some weeks later a young man who had prayed at this meeting, came to Mariano's house to ask if he would type up several hymns. "All the hymnbooks are sold," the young man said, "and I want to give these happy words of comfort to people at the far end of our tribe."

"Brother," said Mariano after he had picked out the hymns, "it is good you want to share the Good New Words with our people. The man who doesn't has only his own interests at heart.

"But before you go, let me tell you one thing more that you can share with those you meet. Don't preach, 'Come to Christ and get a new house,' or 'Come to Christ and have a healthy body.' God never promises us a healthy body or new clothes or big houses. Rather He promises us an eternal goal."

Mariano paused, picked up a tattered manuscript copy of the Chamula New Testament and said, "Brother, I never lived until I heard the message of this Book. I am yet a man with many faults and I have much to learn, but because I take God seriously, I am in the process of succeeding."